A GLIMPSE OF
OUR FATHER:

Lessons Parenthood Reveals
for All of God's Children

By: Quinnise Pettway

Printed in the United States of America
Published & Produced by November Media Publishing

All Scriptures quotations, unless otherwise indicated, are taken from the New American Standard Bible (NASB), King James Version, CJB, Voice, RSV, NIV, EXB.

ISBN-13: 978-1-7354542-7-6

DEDICATION

I would first like to dedicate this book to my Lord and Savior, Jesus Christ. I recognize that it is in you that I live, move, and have my being. Thank you for giving me the vision of this book, and thank you for revealing God, my Heavenly Father in a clearer way. I would also like to dedicate this to my husband Kitrich. Thank you for your support through this journey, and I would not have been able to be a mother to our two amazing daughters without you. I dedicate this to my two beautiful daughters Nia and Brielle. Mommy loves you and I praise God for the gifts that you both are. Thank you for letting me see our Heavenly Father, God through you. My prayer is that as you grow up, you too will see God as your Heavenly Father, and just like my love for you is unconditional, so is His! Last but certainly not least, I dedicate this to my parents Isaac and Eulalia. Thank you both for being awesome examples of God's love for His children in my life. I have never had to doubt your love for me, you have always been there for me, and for that I am truly blessed and grateful!

INTRODUCTION

Upon becoming a parent to my first daughter, God revealed Himself to me in a more profound way as God, my Father. As I listened to comments my daughter made and responses my husband or I gave, I was gently, and sometimes not so gently, reminded of the way the relationship between me and my child mirrored the relationship that my Heavenly Father, God, has with me, His daughter. The Holy Spirit prompted me to just start writing down the revelations every time I or my daughter said something that mimicked the relationship with Our Heavenly Father and His children as I was able to catch a glimpse of Him through our interactions. So, here we are now with A Glimpse of OUR FATHER: Lessons Parenthood Reveals for All of God's Children. Knowing that God IS our Father is something to get excited about because we know that we are in the very best hands. By no means am I implying that we as humans are flawless parents. The revelations received as a parent just scratch the surface of the depth of our perfect parent, God. My desire is that if you are a parent, you will also use your experiences with your children as reminders of God's love for you and your little ones. Even if you are not a parent, this book is for you too, because each of us is someone's child and more importantly, children of the perfect parent, God, so may you be reminded of His love for you too! Overall, the concept of the book is to help all of God's children be reminded of the Father in the Holy Trinity. Very often we talk about the Son and the Holy Spirit, who are absolutely equally important, but we infrequently highlight the awesome and noteworthy character of our unfailing Heavenly Father.

One of the first prayers many learn is what is known as the Lord's Prayer. We start the prayer off with two words, "Our Father" (Matthew 6:9). Many times when we pray and recite scriptures, we simply are saying something we have been taught, recounting words out of tradition, or exclaiming what Momma said, what Daddy said, what our Sunday School teacher said, what our friend said, but not connecting what we are speaking to the depths of our hearts, minds, and souls. We vocalize scriptures and prayers with our mouths but struggle to recognize that the Word of God is living and can be applied to our lives in that very moment, now, and forevermore.

So, back to the two words we speak while opening with the Lord's Prayer, "Our Father." We begin this prayer referencing God as our Father, but have you ever taken the time to think about what that means? Our Father? God? Yes, God! He is our Father. He is my Father, and GOD IS YOUR FATHER TOO! How exciting is that to know that the creator of the entire universe is YOUR faultless, flawless, and loving Heavenly parent who resides with you here on Earth? Ephesians 4:6 reminds us "there is one God and Father of all, who is over all, through all, and in all."

God is our very first parent, as He is our Creator. Jeremiah 1:5 states, "Before I formed you in the womb I knew you, before you were born I set you apart; I appointed you as a prophet to the nations." God knew us even before our earthly parents did. He meticulously crafted us in His mind even before our mortal parents met one another and engaged in the act to physically create us. Our parent, our Father, God, even knew us so much that He numbered the very hairs on our heads (Matthew 10:30). My prayer is that this book encourages you, strengthens you, builds you up, and reminds you just how deeply God, Our Father loves you. He calls you His child according to the first portion of 1 John 3:1 which states, "See what great love the Father has lavished on us, that we should be called children of God!" And that is who we are! We are God's children. Additionally, Romans 8:15-17 states, "For ye have not received the spirit of bondage again to fear; but ye have received the Spirit of adoption, whereby we cry, Abba, Father. The

Spirit itself beareth witness with our spirit, that we are the children of God: And if children, then heirs; heirs of God, and joint-heirs with Christ; if so be that we suffer with him, that we may be also glorified together." This passage is just further confirmation that God is our Father and we are His children. Are you getting excited yet? I hope so, because knowing that God is our Father and we are His children is something to celebrate!

What is a father, some of you might ask? For some, this can be a difficult question to answer depending on upbringing and interaction or lack of interaction with earthly fathers. For those who have not had a positive interaction with earthly fathers or if earthly fathers have passed on, our Heavenly Father has an answer for you in His word. Psalm 65:5 informs us that "God is a father to the fatherless." Psalm 27:10 reminds us that "when my father and my mother forsake me, then the LORD will take me up." These passages also demonstrate God's role not only as Father, but Mother.

Another noteworthy and comforting reference to God is that He is the Great I Am according to Exodus 3:14. That means, whatever you need God to be, HE IS THAT! He is the ultimate parent. He is everything we need Him to be when we need Him to be. Another word of encouragement surrounding God being our Father comes from 1 Corinthians 2:9, "But as it is written, Eye hath not seen, nor ear heard, neither have entered into the heart of man, the things which God hath prepared for them that love Him." God, our Father, has great and mighty things in store for us.

A father gets the name father as a result of becoming a parent. A parent gets the name parent by having children, hence we will explore ways God's love for us has been revealed through my interactions with my children. Matthew 7:9-11 states, "Which of you, if your son asks for bread, will give Him a stone? Or if He asks for a fish will give Him a snake? If you, then, though you are evil know how to give good gifts to your children, how much more will your Father in heaven give good gifts to those who ask Him!" This is a prime reflection of our earthly connection as parents with our Heavenly parent, God. My prayer is that this book will allow you to see that through the revelations I received with interacting with my daughters, God is madly in love with you. He has plans to prosper you and not to harm you, to give you a hope and a future (Jeremiah 29:11). Also note, in the context of this book father can also be synonymous with mother from the perspective of father representing the word parent. God had plans for us even before we were born. He loved us so much that He gave His son for us while we were yet sinners. There is nothing that can or will separate us from the love of God. Our Father's love is eternal. It streams from everlasting to everlasting: translation, forever and ever, which is a mighty long time.

My other hope is that this book will challenge you to be the best son or daughter to our Heavenly Father as He does delight in our obedience to Him and His word. As we desire healthy, whole, and loving relationships with our children and earthly parents, our Heavenly Father, God, desires healthy, whole, and loving relationships with us. He did not leave us without the tools to be able to succeed either. He loved us enough to share the Holy Bible with us as a way to connect with Him and know His mind. Better yet, He IS the Word. John 1:1 reminds us, "in the beginning was the Word, and the Word was with God, and the Word was God." Our Father also loved us enough to give us gifts. As James 1:17 states, "Every good and perfect gift is from above, coming down from the Father of the Heavenly lights, who does not change like shifting shadows." God also reminds us of the gift of His word by sharing in 2 Timothy 3:16-17 that "All scripture is given by inspiration of God, and is profitable for doctrine, for reproof, for correction, for instruction in righteousness: That the man of God may be perfect, thoroughly furnished unto all good works." All of these passages illustrate just how much God loves us as His children, wants a flourishing relationship with us, and wants to communicate His will for our lives.

Now that we have explored what the Word of God reveals about God as our Father, I would like to take time to share lessons I have learned and revelations that have been received by interacting with my daughter, paying attention to her words, and paying attention to my words and reactions. One disclaimer is that I humbly say that by no means can we ever be perfect parents as our Heavenly Father is; nevertheless, we are created in His image and likeness and therefore have the opportunity to imitate Him as parents as Genesis 1:27 states. Similarly, we are all works in progress as His children, and with His help, we are becoming all that He wants us to be, and that is okay. He gives us time to grow. Can I get an "Amen" for our Father's grace, mercy, and willingness to grade on a curve?

Finally, as you proceed, Ephesians 1:17 eloquently articulates my prayer for you. It says, "I keep asking that the God of our Lord Jesus Christ, the glorious Father, may give you the Spirit of wisdom and revelation, so that you may know Him better." This book is designed to be interactive. As you read each section, take a moment to write down your own personal lessons, thoughts, and takeaways in the spaces that are provided. You will be given the opportunity to identify characteristics of your Heavenly Father, journal insights gained, and identify life application principles through the "Reflect and Relate" section, prayers, fill in the blanks and activity charts. Now would be a great time to get a pen, as this is going to be an interactive journey from this point forward. Get ready, set, let's go!

A CHILD'S PERSPECTIVE

Children can say some of the simplest yet most profound remarks. What makes their words so insightful is the fact that they are innocent. They are pure. They say what they mean and mean what they say. They are unfiltered and unrestrained with their speech which can be respectable but at times can be downright piercing. Children do a marvelous job of showing us how we interact and converse with our Heavenly Father whether the communication is conscious or subconscious. No matter what our chronological age is, we are still God's children. Hence, I have a strong inkling (the Holy Spirit) you just might be able to see yourself in the following sections. So now, I invite you to put your spiritual glasses over your natural eyes and see how your vision is transformed as you enter into the revelations gained from the mere words spoken by my child.

Lesson 1

"I DON'T LIKE MY HAIR, AND I WANT IT TO BE STRAIGHT!"

On several occasions, my daughter would declare that she did not like her hair and would much rather that it be straight and "flowy." Her beautiful tight coils did not resemble that of her classmates' hair; hence upon starting a new school, she began to recognize the difference. Despite my husband, her grandparents, and me telling her how beautiful her hair was, she still did not believe it in her heart. Somehow, she started to believe that different was defective or deficient. Also, even though her hair was the same texture as mine, she still had difficulty believing her crown of glory was gorgeous. For a mother, that is particularly tough to hear. The word of God reminds us in Psalm 139: 13-14 "For you created my inmost being; you knit me together in my mother's womb. I praise you because I am fearfully and wonderfully made; your works are wonderful, I know that full well." Genesis 1: 27 also reminds us that "So God created mankind in His own image, in the image of God He created them; male and female He created them." Additionally, the first portion of Genesis 1:31 states, "God saw all that He had made, and it was very good." All of these passages are reminders that because God is our Father and creator, every aspect of us is "good." With and in Him, we lack nothing. We are enough. We are beautiful. We are special. We are all that He wants us to be.

While wanting a different texture of hair might not be your struggle, I am convinced there is something else that the enemy has tried to whisper in your ear, saying something is unattractive, inferior, lacking, or weak. Take a moment to get that area of your life in mind and pray this prayer.

Father God, thank you for creating me in your image. Thank you for reminding me that all that you have made is very good. Thank you for giving me everything that I need. Please help me stop feeling insufficient or inferior in the areas of _____ _____ (fill in the blank) and continue to remind me of all that your word declares that I am. I love you, praise you, and thank you. In the name of Jesus, Amen.

Reflect & Relate Notes

_____

_____

_____

_____

_____

_____

_____

_____

_____

_____

_____

_____

_____

_____

_____

_____

Lesson 2

"MOMMA, I'M SCARED!"

This phrase is a familiar one in my household at bedtime. After tucking my daughter in and engaging in all of our bedtime routine activities, I would attempt to ease out of her room. As soon as I would close the door, I would hear her say, "Momma, I'm scared!" Every parent can relate to hearing their child say this, particularly in the middle of the night. After all, when it is dark, it is hard to see. Many thoughts race through our heads, and light is not in sight. Additionally, there is a certain sense of uncertainty in the darkness. Similarly, at the rumble of thunder and flash of lightning in the middle of the night, the shrieks of fear were belted out. My first reaction was to run to my child's room, pick my daughter up, wrap her in my arms, rub her back, and tell her that everything was going to be okay. I was able to comfort her because I knew there was nothing for her to fear. Even though her room was dark or the thunder and lightning roared and flashed, I knew she was okay because my husband and I were there to protect her and not allow any harm to come her way. I also knew that daylight would be coming in the morning. Our Heavenly Father, God is the same way with us. He is there with and for us.

What is the one concern or multiple matters that you scream in agony to God, "GOD, I'M SCARED!" Where is that darkness that seems like there is no light, lurking in your life? What roaring thunder and flashing lightning are holding you hostage with fear? He reminded me through my daughter, we do not have to fear because He is always with us. Daylight is coming in the morning! He will never leave us or forsake us as Deuteronomy 31:6 states: "Be strong and courageous. Do not be afraid or terrified because of them, for the Lord your God goes with you. He will never leave you nor forsake you." 2 Timothy 1:7 also says that "God has not given us the spirit of fear, but of power, and of love, and of a sound mind."

What fears are you facing today that you need to turn over to your Heavenly Father? Pray this prayer. Dear God, my Father, please help me to cast all of my cares on you because I know that you care for me. Please help me to remember that I have nothing to be scared of because you are with me. You are my light when the world seems so dark. Right now, I give you the fear of _____ (fill in the blank) and ask you to replace that fear with faith, peace, and power. I declare and decree a sound mind no matter what fears come my way. I thank you for the victory over fear. In the name of Jesus, Amen!

REFLECT & RELATE NOTES

_____

_____

_____

_____

_____

_____

_____

_____

_____

_____

_____

_____

_____

_____

_____

_____

Lesson 3

"PICK ME UP."

Particularly when my daughter could not talk or walk well, she would motion for me to pick her up with her arms lifted. As she was able to talk, even though she could walk, she would still sometimes ask for me to pick her up. When she made this request, I did not hesitate to pick her up. Whether it was for me to hold her because she needed the love, attention, and affection, or whether it was for me to help her get from one place to the other, I picked my child up. Also, if she fell, I would pick her up in the midst of her tears. The same is true for our Heavenly Father. He picks us up anytime we call.

When we stretch our hands out to Him for help, He is there. When we fall, Psalm 40:1-2 states, "I waited patiently for the LORD; He turned to me and heard my cry. He lifted me out of the slimy pit, out of the mud and mire; He set my feet on a rock." If you are in a pit, need a touch from the Father, or just need a reminder that He is there, all you have to do right now is ask God, our Father, to pick you up. Stretch out those hands towards Heaven and let Him know that you need Him to lift you. Psalm 145:14 also states, "The LORD upholdeth all that fall, and raiseth up all those that be bowed down." He wants to pick you up!

What are some reasons you need the Father to pick you up?

- Do you need His loving and affectionate pick up?
- Do you need His transporting pick up to help you get from one destination to the other?
- Have you fallen, and need His rescuing pick up?

Pray this prayer. God, my Father, thank you for being a God who picks me up. Thank you for helping take me from one destination to another. Thank you for your loving touch and affection. Right now, I need you to pick me up and carry me through my situation. You know best and I am confident you will carry me through to safety, abundance, and wholeness. I thank you in advance for the victory. In the name of Jesus, Amen.

REFLECT & RELATE NOTES

_____

_____

_____

_____

_____

_____

_____

_____

_____

_____

_____

_____

_____

_____

_____

_____

Lesson 4

"OUCH MOMMA, IT HURTS!"

I heard her screaming and crying as my husband carried her in through the door. She had fallen and scraped her knee on the concrete after running outside in the driveway. The quarter-sized abrasion was bloody and as the blood streamed, so did the tears. I calmly told her that everything would be okay as I proceeded to get the antibiotic ointment, wet towel, and band-aid. As I cleaned her wound, my daughter tearfully stated, "ouch Momma, it hurts!" I hurt as she hurt. I did not like seeing my baby girl injured and in pain, yet I had to clean up her wound and place the healing ointment and bandage on her knee.

Once she was all patched up, we sat on the couch and I allowed her to prop her leg up. Periodically she would cry out, "it hurrrrrrrrts!" I just held her hand and let her know that I understood, but that everything would be okay. I also had to encourage her to stop trying to touch the bandage, as that would make the pain worse. I saw our Heavenly Father reflected through this in that sometimes we fall down. We get hurt. That is part of life. We try to escape pain, but many times, pain is inescapable. Nevertheless, our Father reminds us that He is with us through the hurt and the pain. He also is the healing balm for the cuts, bruises, and scrapes that we get along the way. He is there to hold our hands. He is there to remind us to let the wounds heal and not agitate the wounds by trying to take the bandage off too soon. He is our healer and our Father. Psalms 23:4 reminds us that He walks through the valley of the shadow of death with us. We are also reminded that even though we are God's children, tribulations and trials come, nevertheless, the exciting part is that as John 16:33 states, "These things I have spoken unto you, that in me ye might have peace. In the world ye shall have tribulation: but be of good cheer; I have overcome the world." Our Heavenly Father is a peace giver, a comforter, and an overcomer. He is a healer and companion through all of our pain.

Have you ever felt hurt, wounded, or broken and thought that you were alone? Jot down some areas where you continue to struggle with this_____
_____.

Conversely, can you reflect on times you felt your Heavenly Father's presence through the hurt and the pain? What were those situations? How did He comfort you? Journal your responses in the "Reflect & Relate" section.

Take some time to pray this prayer. Thank you, God, my Father, for always being with me. Thank you for being with me through my hurt, through my pain, and through my bumps and bruises. Thank you for holding my hand and having the healing balm for all of my cuts, scrapes, and wounds. Thank you for being my comforter, peace giver, and ever-present help in time of trouble. Thank you for also reminding me that you are an overcomer, and because I am your child, so am I. I love you and praise you. In the name of Jesus, Amen.

REFLECT & RELATE NOTES

_____

_____

_____

_____

_____

_____

_____

_____

_____

_____

_____

_____

_____

_____

_____

Lesson 5

"Thank you, Momma."

To my surprise, my daughter thanked me for something simple. She thanked me for fixing her dinner. She has also thanked me for doing her hair, putting her clothes on, and giving her a piece of, as she calls it, "fruity gum." These are just a few examples of hearing my child tell me "thank you," but every time she does, those very words coming from her mouth melt my heart. Hearing her say "thank you" never gets old. It also makes me want to do more for her because of her sincere gratitude.

How often do you take the time to give God thanks for all that He has done? Throughout scripture, we are reminded to give thanks to God. Psalm 136:1 states,

"O give thanks unto the LORD; for He is good: for His mercy endureth forever." Psalm 100:4 states, "Enter into His gates with thanksgiving and into His courts with praise: be thankful unto Him, and bless His name." Our Heavenly Father desires our thanks and appreciation.

What are some things you can take the time out to thank God, our Father for? Think about simple and grand things for which you can express your gratitude and envision Him smiling at your thankful heart. Pray this prayer. "Father, God, I just want to take this time to say thank you. Thank you for who you are. Thank you for all that has been done. Thank you for all that you are going to do. Thank you for _____
(fill in the answer to your question). You are truly good and your mercy endures forever. Oh, how I love you. You are truly great and greatly to be praised. In the name of Jesus, Amen!

REFLECT & RELATE NOTES

_____

_____

_____

_____

_____

_____

_____

_____

_____

_____

_____

_____

_____

_____

Lesson 6

"MOMMA, HOW WAS YOUR DAY?"

When I get home from work, in addition to inquiring about my husband's day, I always ask my daughter how her day was. There have been many instances when my daughter beats me to the question. Even before asking me for anything, to take her somewhere, or to give her one of her afterschool treats, she asks, "Momma, how was your day?" This lets me know my daughter is concerned about me, wants to hear from me, and demonstrates she wants a relationship with me. She is not just trying to find out what she can get from me, but she has a desire to know about my well being. Her ear is attuned to what I have to say rather than making a request or telling me about herself. Are you seeing what I am seeing here?

How often are we cultivating our relationship with God by seeking to hear from Him rather than always talking at Him and not listening to what He may have to say to us? How often are we so busy making requests rather than just listening to God? Our Heavenly Father, God, wants a personal relationship with us. No relationship is one-sided, or should I say, no HEALTHY relationship is one-sided where one party does all the talking and requesting. Healthy relationships include both parties talking, listening, and providing feedback. Seeking our Father allows us to draw close to Him. James 4:8 tells us to draw near to God and He will draw near to us. The word also encourages us to abide in the Lord and He will abide in us so that we can bear fruit and represent Him (John 15:4).

What are some ways that you can spend more time enjoying the presence of your Heavenly Father? How can you let Him know that you view your relationship as a two-sided relationship rather than a one-sided association? Journal your responses in the "Reflect & Relate" section.

Pray this prayer. Heavenly Father, I love you. I enjoy your presence. I want to be in your presence, bask in your glory, and be filled with your spirit. Please forgive me for the times that I get so busy doing all of the talking, demanding, complaining, and requesting. Help me to listen more in our time together. Help remove all distractions and hindrances to our communion. I love You and thank you for being an amazing Father who loves me and wants a relationship with me through prayer and through the study of your word. In the name of Jesus, Amen.

REFLECT & RELATE NOTES

_____

_____

_____

_____

_____

_____

_____

_____

_____

_____

_____

_____

_____

_____

_____

Lesson 7

"BUT I'M NOT SLEEPY; I DON'T WANT TO GO TO BED NOW."

I am certain that every parent can relate to hearing his or her child say this over a half a million times. We know our child has been up past his or her normal bedtime, has had an extremely busy day, or has missed his or her regular naptime. When these potentially catastrophic occurrences happen, they get cranky, irritable, and outright irrational. Despite seeing the yawns, fatigue, and lethargy, they still insist that they are not sleepy. Our little ones may even go as far as to begin to snooze in the car, on the couch, or sprawl out on the floor, but immediately when trying to take them to bed, they awaken with the very words, "I'm not sleepy. I don't want to go to bed now."

As I watched my daughter display these behaviors, I was reminded of how this very circumstance applies to me as a child of God. Sometimes we need to rest, take a break, get away, or just flat out SIT DOWN SOMEWHERE! How many times do we get caught up in being so busy that we don't realize that we need a break? From taking care of the household, working full time, tending to children's needs, meeting our spouse's needs, participating in ministry, the list goes on and on... we need a break! We get burnt out. We become cranky, have a bad attitude, are not executing our gifts and talents to our fullest potential, and the excellence that is deserved because we are trying to operate in the flesh and not through the spirit, and we just need to take time to rest.

Willpower, white-knuckling it, and faking it until we make it just will not do. Our Heavenly Father did not call us to operate that way AT ALL! As Psalm 23:2 references, "He maketh me to lie down in green pastures and He leadeth me beside the still waters." Sometimes our Heavenly Father has to force us to take a break through sickness, job loss, natural disasters, and other unexpected trials. Let us try not to get to the point where we have to be made to lie down, but rather recognize some of the warning signs to take some time to rest. Even God rested as Genesis 2:2 states, "And on the seventh day God ended His work which He had made; and He rested on the seventh day from all His work which He had made." If God rested, what more does that say about us and our need for rest? Yes, I am talking to you; you are not exempt!

Are you overcommitted, overwhelmed, or overworked? Do you find yourself more depressed, irritable, or stressed than usual? If you answered yes, perhaps there are some activities from which you need to break. Take a moment and say this prayer. Dear Heavenly Father, I first would like to thank you for being a God of rest. Thank you that I can find rest in you. Thank you for allowing me to find restoration and refreshment in you. You remind me in Psalm 23 that after you make me to lie down in green pastures and lead me beside the still waters, you restore my soul! Right now, I ask that you reveal any areas, situations, circumstances, or commitments from which I need to rest. Show me where I need to take a break. Please help me to lie down in green pastures and lead me beside the still waters. Please restore my soul. I thank you for revealing these areas to me, and thank you for complete wholeness as I am obedient to your prompting to rest. In the name of Jesus, Amen!

REFLECT & RELATE ACTIVITY: STOP, REST, REFLECT, AND RESTORE WARNING CHART

5 warning signs that I am getting burned out:

1._____

2._____

3._____

4._____

5._____

3 accountability partners to help me identify when I need to regain balance:

1._____

2._____

3._____

5 actions I can take to restore, refresh, and relax:

1._____

2._____

3._____

4._____

5._____

Lesson 8

"I WANT THAT OTHER FRUIT SNACK."

One of my daughter's favorite treats is fruit snacks. One day while sitting at the kitchen table, my husband asked her if he could have one of her fruit snacks. Yes, I said, just one. You would have thought that he asked for the entire package due to her adamant response of "NO!" Thoughts came to mind of the importance of sharing and not being selfish. After all, she did have the entire bag of snacks for herself. Has anyone put the mirror up? Does this sound familiar to us as adults? How often do we withhold things from our Heavenly Father due to wanting to keep them all to ourselves? Finances, gifts, talents, time, and other areas of our lives are all used for our selfish gain and desire rather than giving and sharing, which is the desire of our Father, God.

God reminds us to give to others, to give and it shall be given unto us, to give cheerfully rather than grudgingly or of necessity, and that it is more blessed to give than to receive. 2 Corinthians 9:6-8 states, "But this I say, He which soweth sparingly shall reap also sparingly; and He which soweth bountifully shall reap also bountifully. Every man according as He purposeth in His heart, so let Him give; not grudgingly, or of necessity: for God loveth a cheerful giver. And God is able to make all grace abound toward you; that ye, always having all sufficiency in all things, may abound to every good work." Giving reflects our Heavenly Father's very image. After all, He gave us all the ultimate gift, His ONLY Son, Jesus Christ. Even when we think of the concept of tithing, God only asks us for ten percent. He allows us to maintain the other ninety percent. That sounds like a good Father to me!

How often do we withhold this from our Father? What might you be holding back where you know the Father has been prompting you to give? Is it your time? Is it your talent? Is it your finances? Take some time to pray this prayer. Dear God, my Father, first I want to thank you for your grace and mercy. Thank you for setting the ultimate example of giving, by giving your only Son for me. The least I can do is give back to you what you have given me. I humbly ask for your forgiveness for all that I have withheld from you because I realize that it is yours. Please give me the strength, courage, and wisdom to give freely and fully. I love you and give your name all of the praise. In the name of Jesus, Amen!

REFLECT & RELATE ACTIVITY: I'VE BEEN HOLDING BACK.

Three areas I have been holding back from God

1._____

2._____

3._____

Three ways that I can release what I have been holding back from God

1._____

2._____

3._____

Lesson 9

"I WANT TO WEAR MY PINK SHIRT."

My daughter's favorite color is pink. She loves pink shirts, pink pants, pink toys, and pink everything! She went through a phase where she ONLY wanted to wear pink shirts. Now, of course, her wardrobe consists of an array of colors and is not simply limited to pink. Nevertheless, when I tried to dress her in any color other than pink, she would pitch a fit. I clearly remember one morning that I was getting her dressed for school. She was still asleep as I put her clothes on. This particular morning, I was putting a yellow shirt on her. After all, she looks gorgeous in more than just one color! As she opened her eyes, she started crying and trying to take the shirt off, stating, "I want to wear my pink shirt."

As I kept trying to put the shirt over her head, she kept trying to pull the shirt off her head. Oftentimes we do the same thing to our Heavenly Father. Whether it is wanting to remain in the same deadbeat relationships out of comfort and familiarity or it is staying at that job that is leading us on the fast track to a heart attack or stroke, but we are staying there due to thinking and believing that there are no better options, we keep trying to take that yellow shirt off because we only want the pink shirt.

God has more in store my friends! There is more that God has for us than just the pink shirt. Blue might be your color, or even a little green. Oftentimes, we limit ourselves by only seeing things through our lenses, when God has far greater things in store for us. The first portion of Isaiah 43:19 states, "Behold, I will do a new thing; now it shall spring forth; shall ye not know it?" He wants to do new things in our lives. Also, Isaiah 55:9-8 states, "For my thoughts are not your thoughts, neither are your ways my ways, saith the LORD." 1 Corinthians 2:9 also states, "But as it is written, Eye hath not seen, nor ear heard, neither have entered into the heart of man, the things which God hath prepared for them that love Him." There is so much more that our Heavenly Father has in store for you so go ahead and TAKE THE LIMITS OFF! "For as the heavens are higher than the earth, so are my ways higher than your ways, and my thoughts than your thoughts," says our Father in Isaiah 55:9. My brothers and sisters, let us embrace ALL that our Father has for us and not be hindered by our comfort zones and tiny boxes.

In what areas are you limiting your Heavenly Father? What are you holding on to that you need to let go of? Pray this prayer. Dear God, My Father. The statement is true that you know best. After all, you did create me. You see all, hear all, know, all, and have all power. Help me to trust you more. Help me to let go of the things that I am holding on to that are not for my good or that are just limiting me. Dismantle the boxes that I have created in my own life. Take me out of my comfort zone and help me to cling on to the unfamiliar territory that you have prepared for me. Clothe me in what you see fit. Help me to embrace all that you have for me because I know you have great things in store for me. You want to do a new thing in my life, and I want to be ready. Thank you for continuing to be patient with me as I go through this process of letting go, taking off the old, and putting on the new. You are good. You are wise. You are mighty. I love you and praise you. I wait in eager expectation for all that you are going to do in my life and praise you for all that you have already done. In the name of Jesus, Amen.

REFLECT & RELATE NOTES

_____

_____

_____

_____

_____

_____

_____

_____

_____

_____

_____

_____

_____

_____

_____

_____

Lesson 10

"I AM NOT AS SMART AS THEM."

It broke my heart to hear these words come out of my daughter's mouth. Let me take a moment to put this into context. She had just had her birthday and has twin godsisters who are 10 months older than her. When I explained that they were going to be 5 and no longer 4 (she had just become 4), she equated them being older with them being smarter. Crocodile tears fell from her eyes as she exclaimed, "I am not as smart as them." I rubbed her back, wiped her eyes, and began reminding her of who she was. I also attempted, the best way I could, in terms that a four-year-old could understand, to explain why there was no reason she needed to compare herself to her godsisters. Once again, my Psalm 139 alarm bell went off. "I will praise thee because I am fearfully and wonderfully made. Marvelous are thy works" (Psalms 139).

You are smart. You are enough. You are who God says you are and not who you feel or think you are. You are how Mommy and Daddy see you. You are brilliant. You are gifted. You are talented. These were all the phrases that flowed from my mouth to my child. Oh, how it broke my heart when I heard my daughter utter these words and express feelings of inferiority at such a young age, as tears streamed down her beautiful little face. I caught a glimpse of our Father through this encounter with my child. How many times do we doubt who our Heavenly Father says that we are? How many times do we forget that we are made in His image and likeness, and that is enough? We do not have to compare ourselves to anyone else, and we are all awesome and amazing in our own unique ways. We have gifts and talents that God has only equipped us to carry out.

When is the last time you doubted your worth? Have you been questioning your value lately? To whom have you been comparing yourself? Whose social media page do you need to take a break from because you have found yourself getting down every time you see their life story told in photographs, or do you need to fast from social media as a whole? Take time to pray this prayer. Father God, I want to thank you for reminding me of who I am in you. Thank you for reminding me that I am worthwhile. I am smart enough. I am gifted. I do have talents. I do not have to compare myself to anyone because you created me uniquely with divine design and purpose. Please forgive me for forgetting or struggling to believe that I am who you say that I am. I wait in eager expectation for all that you will continue to do through me, and I rest in complete confidence that I can do all things through you. Thank you for reminding me of these truths Heavenly Father. In the name of Jesus, AMEN.

REFLECT & RELATE ACTIVITY: GOD SAYS THAT I AM...

Read the scripture and write down who God says that you are based on the passage.

Genesis 1:26-27 &, 31	
Deuteronomy 28:1-14	
Psalm 139:14	
Isaiah 43:4	
Isaiah 53:5	
Matthew 5:1-16	
John 3:16	

John 15:5	
2 Corinthians 5:17	
Galatians 4:7	
Ephesians 2:10	
1 Peter 2:9	

Lesson 11

"MOMMA, I DON'T WANT TO BE PATIENT. I DO NOT LIKE BEING PATIENT!"

So, one of my daughter's pastimes is to go to the park and play. My husband and I had promised her that she could go to the park one particular day, but we told her that she would have to wait. We had some other tasks that we needed to get done around the house before we went to the park, but we were certainly planning to keep our word and take her to the park. What seemed like every two minutes, my daughter would ask, "is it time to go to the park yet?" We would reply, with "no, not yet." The more she asked, the more we explained that she would need to be patient and wait. It was at this point that she exclaimed, "Momma, I don't want to be patient. I DO NOT LIKE BEING PATIENT!"

I had to chuckle when I heard my daughter say these words because she did nothing but remind me when my Heavenly Father has made a promise to me or answered yes to one of my prayers, but I did not see the manifestation of the promise immediately. How often do we get into a foot-stomping, arms flailing, voice hollering two-year-old tantrum with God when He tells us to wait or to be patient? The promise will be fulfilled. The prayer has already been answered with a yes, but oftentimes we have to exercise patience until the promise comes to pass. Psalms 27:14 states that we are to "Wait on the LORD: be of good courage, and He shall strengthen thine heart: wait, I say, on the LORD." Romans 8:24 also states, "But if we hope for what we do not yet have, we wait for it patiently." Isaiah 40: 31 also says, "But they that wait upon the LORD shall renew their strength; they shall mount up with wings as eagles; they shall run, and not be weary; and they shall walk, and not faint." The common themes in each passage are waiting, patience and assurance that our strength can be renewed during the wait.

What is something you have been struggling to wait on the Lord for? What type of attitude have you had during the wait? While waiting can be quite a challenge, pray this prayer. Heavenly Father, thank you for the

fact that I can come to you with all of my cares and concerns. Thank you for always having a listening ear. Right now, I need your strength to endure as I strive to wait patiently on you for _____.
You remind me in James 1:3 "that the trying of my faith worketh patience." I know that you hear my prayers and I thank you in advance for renewing my strength and for the manifestation of your promises. You are good and worthy to be praised. In the name of Jesus, AMEN!

REFLECT & RELATE NOTES

_____

_____

_____

_____

_____

_____

_____

_____

_____

_____

_____

_____

_____

_____

Lesson 12

"GIVE ME MY TEDDY BACK."

One bedtime routine I had with my daughter was to pray, tuck her in, and sing a few praise and worship songs as she went to sleep. One night, while lying on the floor next to her bed in preparation to sing, as I usually do, she kept throwing her teddy bear out of the bed at me. By the third time, of getting hit with the bear, I took the teddy bear and put it on the side of her bed. A few moments later, my daughter stated "Mommy, give me back my teddy. Where did you put him?"

I told her I was not going to give her teddy bear back because she kept throwing teddy out of the bed. I explained that once she was ready to receive the teddy back by being respectful and obedient, I would give the teddy back, but there were some actions that she was required to display to demonstrate that she was ready. As we began to sing our worship songs, she would periodically ask where teddy was and if she could have him back. While in the back of my mind I knew that I was going to give him back, I told her she would need to just wait. I had her explain why Teddy was taken away in the first place. She reluctantly repeated back to me "because I kept throwing Teddy at you." Finally, once all of our songs were sung and she apologized again for throwing Teddy out of the bed at me, I gave him back to her. Hebrews 12:6 reminds us that the Lord disciplines those He loves because He wants us to do better and be better. For my child, not giving Teddy back right away was to help her appreciate her cuddly friend.

How often do we take things for granted that our Heavenly Father has given us and it takes having the very blessing that we took for granted being taken away to realize the value? How often do we have to experience some form of discipline that does not feel pleasant at the time in order to appreciate all that God has given us? Our Father wants to bless us. He has plans to prosper us, not harm us, to give us a hope and a future as Jeremiah 29:11 states, but we should not take His blessings for granted. What is something you have been taking for granted lately? Is it your spouse, your children, your job, your home, or your finances? Is it your health? Whatever it is, get that in your mind and pray this prayer. Father God, I thank you for being a merciful God. I ask that you forgive me for taking so many things for granted and misusing the very gifts that you have given me. Please bring to my attention anyone or anything I have taken for granted and help me to appreciate all that you have given me. I praise you and thank you for the revelation that is to come. In the name of Jesus, Amen.

REFLECT & RELATE ACTIVITY: TAKEN FOR GRANTED NO MORE!

People, places, or things that I have taken for granted	Action steps to show appreciation

Lesson 13

"I DON'T WANT TO GIVE MY LITTLE SISTER MY TUTU!"

As we were preparing for the arrival of our second daughter, my older daughter noticed some items in her closet that I was saving for her little sister. When she spotted a cute little pink tutu shirt, I excitedly shared that it would be for her little sister. She was not happy to hear that news. I explained that she had outgrown the tutu so it was no longer useful to her. She proceeded to try to put the tutu on. I gently reminded her that it was now too small, but that she would be able to get a new one or one that was a better fit, but this one was now for her sister. I tried explaining to my daughter, as her eyes were filled with tears, it is great to be able to share with her sister and let go of some of her old things because that means that new things can also come her way. Once again, I had to giggle as I recognized the message God our Father was trying to teach me through the pink tutu experience. There are times to let go of things that we hold on to. They are no longer a fit. They are more of a detriment than a benefit. Ecclesiastes 3:1, 6 states, "To everything there is a season, and a time to every purpose under the heaven: A time to get, and a time to lose; a time to keep, and a time to cast away."

Take a moment to take inventory of your own closet (literally and figuratively). What are you holding on to that it is time to donate? What is too tight, too small, or just outright does not fit into your life at this point? Take time now to pray this prayer. Dear Father God, I thank you for all you have given me. Thank you for reminding me that there are seasons for everything in my life. Please open my eyes to see what I need to clean out of my literal and figurative closets. Please reveal the relationships, habits, attitudes, and mindsets that I need to purge so that I can make room for the new things that you want to do in my life. Thank you for hearing my prayer and opening my eyes and ears to see and hear what you have planned for me in this season. In the name of Jesus, Amen.

REFLECT & RELATE ACTIVITY: CLOSET CLEANOUT

God, I need to purge…	Action steps

Lesson 14

"BUT MOMMY, I WANT TO GO SOMEWHERE ELSE. WHERE ELSE ARE WE GOING?"

My daughter loves to be on the go. She is by no means a homebody. At bedtime, oftentimes she asks where we are going to go the next day or what the plans are for the following week. Each time she asks, I answer. Particularly on weekends, she enjoys going to the local warehouse store to get all of the yummy snacks, stop by the sample machine, and eat all of the latest and greatest samples that are provided in the store. She also enjoys exploring the big box store to get our groceries and the mall so that she can play in the play area and go through all of the toy stores.

One day, after doing all of her favorite activities and making all of her favorite stops, she asked "Momma, where else are we going? I want to go somewhere else; I do not want to go home." Thoughts came to mind of my child being ungrateful that we had just done all of the things she enjoyed, and yet she was still asking for more, appearing to be unsatisfied. Her words and thoughts convicted me and reminded me of times when my Heavenly Father has blessed me over and over again, but for some reason I seem to forget, take the blessings for granted, fail to bask in His goodness and blessings because I am so busy looking for the next blessing, next victory, or next breakthrough. We must take time to thank our Father for all that He has done, be grateful for our many blessings, and reflect on our answered prayers. This does not mean that we cannot ask our Father for things and expect that He will do great things for us, but we must not forget that He has already done so much for us!

We need not complain and grumble as the children of Israel did in Exodus 11:1, "Now the people complained about their troubles in the hearing of the Lord. When the Lord heard it, His anger burned. The fire of the Lord burned among them, and destroyed some around the outer parts of the tents." Yes, they were in the wilderness, but God had just delivered them out of the hands of Pharaoh via PARTING THE RED SEA. They witnessed their enemies drown in the very sea that they passed through with dry ground underneath their feet. Also, even in the wilderness, they were fed daily and their attire did not become worn. Instead of complaining, give thanks. Psalm 103:2 states, "Bless the LORD, O my soul, and forget not all His benefits." Psalms 77:11 also states, "I will remember the deeds of the LORD; yes, I will remember your miracles of long ago."

In what areas of your life have you found yourself complaining or experiencing ingratitude? What victories do you need to reflect upon so that you are reminded of the goodness of our Father? Take a moment to reflect and then pray this prayer. Father God, thank you for your many blessings. Thank you for all of the victories that I have seen in my life thus far. You keep blessing me over and over again, and for that, I must express my gratitude. Please forgive me for sometimes getting caught up in consuming and receiving more rather than remembering and praising you for the blessings I have received. Help me not to forget all that you have already done in times where I find myself looking for the next blessing, breakthrough, or victory. I love you with all of my heart and give you all of the glory, honor, and praise for my life. I will bless the Lord at all times: His praise shall be continually in my mouth as Psalm 34:1 states. In the name of Jesus, Amen.

REFLECT & RELATE ACTIVITY

I encourage you to make a "Blessings List." Put it up somewhere that you can see and add to it as often as possible. When you feel like complaining, look at the list, and if you still feel like complaining or questioning God's work in your life, add five more items to the list.

"Bless the LORD, O my soul, and forget not all His benefits."

Psalm 103:2

1. _____

2. _____

3. _____

4. _____

5. _____

Lesson 15

"DADDY IS MAD AT MEEEEEEEE!"

A s you have seen from previous statements made by my daughter, a good portion of her insightful and relatable statements happen just after bath time. This is true for this scenario as well. My husband and I had asked my daughter to follow directions after getting changed into her PJs. We asked her to get down on her knees, as we do every night to engage in our evening prayer together. This particular night, she decided she wanted to jump on her bed instead. In a soft tone, both my husband and I took turns asking her to get down on her knees, as the two of us were doing, yet she continued to jump. My husband finally very sternly stated, "GET ON YOUR KNEES NOW!"

As she burst into tears, she conceded and got down on her knees. Between tears and sniffles, she began to say and complete her evening prayer. As part of our routine, I would remain in her room for a little while longer to sing a few praise and worship songs. My husband would turn out the light and close the door. Once he left and I started to sing, periodically, my child would blurt out in a sad and tearful tone "Daddy is mad at meeeeeeeee!" I assured her that her father was not mad at her. He was trying to get her attention and wanted her to be obedient because he and I knew she was very capable of doing so. Still, as I continued to sing, moments later she would blurt out in tears, "Ahhhh, Daddy is mad at meeeeeeeee!"

A few times after saying that, she asked if I could ask her father to come in so that she could tell him that she was sorry. I also explained that Daddy was not mad but did not like the fact that she had been disobedient and not listened to his request. I encouraged her to also explain, once he came in, the reason that she was sorry. I called my husband in the room. In a soft voice, she told her daddy she was sorry for not listening and getting on her knees when he asked. In just as gentle of a voice, my husband told her that it was okay, he forgave her, he was not mad at her, and he proceeded to embrace his daughter. I picture our Heavenly Father, God, doing the same thing to and for us. Did you catch a glimpse of Him too? When we find ourselves feeling unworthy because we have sinned against Him, feeling as if we cannot talk to Him, feeling riddled with shame and guilt, all we have to do is cry out to Him and ask for forgiveness.

He is faithful to forgive us. 1 John 1:9 reminds us, "If we confess our sins, He is faithful and just to forgive us *our* sins, and to cleanse us from all unrighteousness." He loves us. He longs to embrace us. He has freed us from all condemnation, guilt, and shame. We do have to confess and turn from those sins, but He loves us unconditionally. Remember, God, Our Father loved us so much that He sent His ONLY son to die for our sins so that we could have everlasting life and have access to Him (John 3:16). Now that is what you call a loving father!

What thoughts are holding you captive and having you think that God is mad at you? What sins have you felt are too big to forgive? Upon answering the questions, take a moment to pray this prayer. Thank you, Father God, for loving me unconditionally. Thank you that nothing separates me from your love and forgiveness. I do confess_____ (fill in the blank) and ask that you forgive and cleanse me from all unrighteousness because I love you with my whole heart. I want to live a life pleasing unto you. You are so good, and I thank you that your mercy endures forever. In the name of Jesus, Amen.

REFLECT & RELATE ACTIVITY

Now that you have prayed your prayer, I encourage you to go one step further. Write those sins on a sheet of paper, tear it into tiny pieces, and place them in the trash can. I pray that this is a freeing experience for you. After completing the activity, take some time to reflect and relate in the space below.

_____

_____

_____

_____

_____

_____

_____

_____

_____

_____

Lesson 16

"SO WHEN AM I GOING TO BE FIVE?"

The garage door had barely come down after getting home from her fourth birthday party at the place with the singing mascot and plethora of games when the aforementioned question was posed. We had not even unloaded her birthday gifts from the trunk before my child was already ready to zoom past age four to age five. Her statement brought me to the thought of being content. Philippians 4:11-12 states, "I am not saying this because I am in need, for I have learned to be content whatever the circumstances. I know what it is to be in need, and I know what it is to have plenty. I have learned the secret of being content in any and every situation, whether well fed or hungry, whether living in plenty or in want." We must take time to enjoy the journey regardless of the situation we are in. We must work to appreciate the journey rather than always focusing on the next destination or milestone.

Take a moment to reflect on where you are in life now. What can you be content with, in this season? What is important to enjoy and reflect upon now? In what ways do you need to slow down, and be content? Pray this prayer. Dear Heavenly Father, thank you for my current situation. Thank you for all that you have done and given me thus far in my life. Please open my eyes to see you in this season and help me to experience contentment even right now. Please forgive me for trying to rush through life rather than enjoying this awesome journey that you have me going through. I thank you and praise you for your continued goodness, grace, and mercy. In the name of Jesus, Amen.

Reflect & Relate Notes

_____

_____

_____

_____

_____

_____

_____

_____

_____

_____

_____

_____

_____

Lesson 17

"BUT I WANTED THE MICKEY MOUSE COLORING BOOK AND CRAYONS!"

My daughter's Vacation Bible School teachers allowed their students to pick a prize out of the treasure box each night at the end of class. When I went to pick her up from class, I noticed she had a beautiful butterfly that was encased in plastic along with flowers. The treasure was solar-powered, and if we placed it in the sun, the butterfly would fly around in the plastic case above the flowers. I thought it was a pretty cool prize if you ask me, but that was not the case for Miss Nia.

When I exclaimed how pretty the butterfly garden was, she erupted into tears and hung her head down. When I asked what was wrong, she exclaimed, "but I wanted the Mickey Mouse coloring book and crayons, but Noah got to it before me!"

I tried explaining how nifty her prize was, but she was not trying to hear it. The tears did cease when we got into the car and as we drove home, but they resurfaced at bedtime. She loudly howled out, "but Momma, I wanted the Mickey Mouse coloring book and crayons, but Noah got it before me!" I did validate her feelings of sadness and disappointment by letting her know that it is okay to feel sad, but I also encouraged her surrounding the beauty of the butterfly garden gift she received. I told her that we could put it out in the sun in the morning so that she could see the butterfly in action. None of my words seemed to console my heartbroken child. Even after I kissed her goodnight and left her room, I could hear her crying until she fell asleep. The next morning, guess what she did? She actually asked if we could put her butterfly in the sun!

Like my child, how often have we as God's children been disappointed when we did not get a gift, talent, item, or object that someone else received? How often have we wanted to trade in our gifts and talents for the talents of others? How often have we perceived others as receiving better blessings than us, as opposed to just pausing and pondering on the gifts and blessings our Heavenly Father has given us? God does understand if we get sad, frustrated, and upset, however, He does not want us to stay there. He wants us to recognize the gifts and talents that He specifically designed and meticulously tailored to us. Yes, He loves us that much that He uniquely made us and gave us gifts according to His plan and thoughts. 1 Corinthians 12:4 states, "Now there are diversities of gifts, but the same Spirit." Verses 8-10 state, "For to one is given by the Spirit the word of wisdom; to another the word of knowledge by the same Spirit; To another faith by the same Spirit; to another the gifts of healing by the same Spirit; To another the working of miracles; to another prophecy; to another discerning of spirits; to another divers kind of tongues; to another the interpretation of tongues:" Verse 28 states, "And God hath set some in the church, first apostles, secondarily prophets, thirdly teachers, after that miracles, then gifts of healings, helps, governments, diversities of tongues." All of the gifts that our Heavenly Father gives us are for His glory and His honor. Regardless of the gift, each is valuable and should be viewed as such in contrast to meditating on the blessings, gifts, and talents that we do not possess.

Are there any talents or gifts that you see your brother or sister have that you have hoped for or prayed for? Have there been times that you wished for the blessings or provisions your neighbor has and failed to look at and appreciate the gifts our Heavenly Father has given you? Take the time to pray this prayer. Father God, I love you. I thank you for the blessings, gifts, and talents that you have given me. Please forgive me for the times where I have spent my energy wishing and hoping for the blessings, gifts, provisions, and talents of others when you have already given me gifts and talents that are unique to me. I praise you and I am glad that you reminded me that what you have for me, is for me. All that you have given me is enough and I want to use the gifts that you have given me for your glory. You are awesome and worthy of my praise. In the name of Jesus, Amen.

Reflect & Relate Activity: My Gifts and Talents

My strengths

1._____

2._____

3._____

My talents

1._____

2._____

3._____

My spiritual gifts

1._____

2._____

3._____

My passions

1._____

2._____

3._____

Others come to me for or say that I am good at

1._____

2._____

3._____

Lesson 18

"WHERE ARE WE GOING TOMORROW, AND THE NEXT DAY, AND THE NEXT DAY, AND THE NEXT DAY?"

As you may know from previous readings, my daughter is inquisitive and likes to be on the move! One day, as I was driving her to daycare, she posed the question "Where are we going tomorrow?" I responded with the plans for the next day. She then continued to inquire about the next day, the next day, the next day, and the next day. I had to giggle as she asked because it made me think of how we treat our

Heavenly Father and inquire about the future. I told my daughter, "Let's just enjoy today, tomorrow, and the following day." After all, I had already revealed our plans for the entire weekend.

How often does God reveal parts of our future to us, but we are still dissatisfied with that peek into the future and want to know more? Probably too many times to count on both hands I bet. We must trust in Him and know that He has our lives in His hands. We must be confident that even if we do not know all of the plans that He has in store for us, He does have plans and will reveal those plans in His timing.

Matthew 6:25-34 states, "Therefore I say unto you, Take no thought for your life, what ye shall eat, or what ye shall drink; nor yet for your body, what ye shall put on. Is not the life more than meat, and the body than raiment? Behold the fowls of the air: for they sow not, neither do they reap, nor gather into barns; yet your Heavenly Father feedeth them. Are ye not much better than they? Which of you by taking thought can add one cubit unto His stature? And why take ye thought for raiment? Consider the lilies of the field, how they grow; they toil not, neither do they spin: And yet I say unto you, That even Solomon in all His glory was not arrayed like one of these. Wherefore, if God so clothe the grass of the field, which today is, and tomorrow is cast into the oven, shall He not much more clothe you, O ye of little faith? Therefore take no thought, saying, What shall we eat? or, What shall we drink? or, Wherewithal shall we be clothed? (For after all these things do the Gentiles seek:) for your Heavenly Father knoweth that ye have need of all these things. But seek ye first the kingdom of God, and His righteousness; and all these things shall be added unto you. Take therefore no thought for the morrow: for the morrow shall take thought for the things of itself. Sufficient unto the day is the evil thereof."

There was an abundance of wisdom in that passage, right? In summary, our Heavenly Father wants us to focus on today and be certain that He will take care of everything that follows. Since He tends to the needs of even the birds, He will surely meet our needs as His children.

Are there areas in your life where you are struggling to be patient surrounding further revelation? Are there parts of your future that have been revealed, but others Father God has yet to share? Take a moment to pray this prayer. Father God, thank you that I can place my hope and trust in you. Thank you for having my life in your hands and thank you that I can be confident that you know what is best for me. Thank you for reminding me that if I seek your first and your righteousness, all these things will be added to me. Help me to trust you more and seek you more. Help me to not worry about the future, because I know that my life is in your hands. Please forgive me for the times I struggle with anxiety, impatience, and lack of faith. Please forgive me when I have failed to seek you first. I love you, thank you, and praise you. In the name of Jesus, Amen.

REFLECT & RELATE NOTES

_____

_____

_____

_____

_____

_____

_____

_____

_____

_____

_____

_____

_____

_____

Lesson 19

"MOMMY, SHE HIT ME AND WILL NOT LET THE OTHER GIRLS PLAY WITH ME."

My daughter started a new school for pre-kindergarten. Some of the children had attended the school before her and had already formed relationships. One day, she came home crying and stated that one of the little girls would not play with her, nor would she let the other girls play with her. Another day, shortly after that announcement, she stated that the same child hit her in the face with her elbow. Now all of you reading this know that this information sent my blood boiling and at the same time broke my heart.

I immediately went in to defend and protect mode. I discussed the issue with her teacher. To make a long story short, her teacher first stated that my four-year-old could play with other children, that she could tell her classmate she did not like the fact that she hit her in the face with her elbow (so that she could learn how to speak up for herself), and she stated that my child had not told her these incidents had occurred. While I am all for children learning to speak up for themselves and gaining assertiveness skills, this was an example of a parental intervention being necessary, especially because the adult who was supposed to be in charge seemed to lack concern.

Attempting to isolate my child from the other girls and hitting her in the face with an elbow is never appropriate. I voiced this concern to the teacher. By the end of the conversation, the teacher did say that she would talk with the other child's parents surrounding the matters and keep an eye on the two. I continued to check in with my child to make sure the behaviors had stopped after talking with her teacher. Praise God, the issue did get resolved and there were no further incidents. God, our Father, is the same with us. His word clearly states in 2 Chronicles 20:15 He said: "Listen, King Jehoshaphat and all who live in Judah and Jerusalem! This is what the LORD says to you: 'Do not be afraid or discouraged because of this vast army. For the battle is not yours, but God's.'"

What battles are you facing today that you need to stand still and let your Father fight for you? He will fight our battles, and guess what, He has never lost which means YOU WILL WIN EVERY TIME! Just like I went to battle for my earthly child without hesitation, our Heavenly Father goes to battle for you. Has there ever been a time where you thought that you had to take matters into your own hands or that your Father, God would not fight your battle for you? Take a moment to pray this prayer. Dear Heavenly Father, thank you for reminding me that these battles that I face are not mine. They are yours! You fight for me. Right now, I cast all of my cares on you. I pray that you take control in _____ (name your battles) and replace my fear, discouragement, and anxiety with your peace that surpasses all understanding. I am victorious in you and for that, I give you praise. In the name of Jesus, Amen.

REFLECT & RELATE ACTIVITY: BATTLES GOD HAS ALREADY FOUGHT AND WON IN MY LIFE

1. _____

2. _____

3. _____

Lesson 20

"TOMORROW IS GOING TO BE A VERY BAD DAY."

On October 31st, my daughter's school went all out for the holiday. The children had the opportunity to dress up, play games, trick or treat at school, and party, party, party. In addition to that, our church was hosting Halleluiah Night which included more fellowship, food, and fun. On the eve of October 31st, my daughter declared that "tomorrow would be a very, very good day," and expressed sheer excitement to go to school and church to show off her cupcake costume and par-tay.

Once that day (very long day, I must add) came to an end, she professed that "tomorrow is going to be a very bad day." My daughter's thought process amazed me in that she recognized that November 1st would likely be an average day, rather than a day full of parties, parties, and more parties. As adults, I know we can relate to this feeling as well. Whether it is returning home from a fabulous vacation, celebrating our wedding day, or experiencing the joy of a new baby, you can fill in the blank of those "natural high" days from which we do not want to come down. Also, we could have even attended a mountaintop experience in which we engaged at a church service, conference, or retreat. We just do not want to come back to reality. We want to stay engulfed in bliss, freedom, glee, and the glory of God continually. We want the excitement to last forever. We do not want to return to the routine and monotony of life.

While trying to minister to my daughter when she experienced this thought process, three scripture passages came to mind. The first passage, "This is the day which the LORD hath made; we will rejoice and be glad in it" is a reminder that our Heavenly Father desires that we rejoice daily, Psalm 118:24. Every day we have the opportunity to wake up on this side of Heaven is a blessing. Even in the routine days, we still have blessings to count and things for which to be grateful. Secondly, Lamentations also reminds us that, "It is of the LORD's mercies that we are not consumed because His compassions fail not. They are new every morning: great is thy faithfulness," Lamentations 3:22-23. Our Father's mercies are new every morning. We should start expecting that great things will happen every day, because the fact that we have the opportunity to experience new mercies every morning, is enough to shout! Lastly, Psalm 23:6 says, "Surely goodness and mercy shall follow me all the days of my life: and I will dwell in the house of the Lord forever." This verse lets us know that we can expect goodness and mercy every day, not just one day, or some days. This reminder is worth a praise break even right now (cue the music!). Furthermore, I was reminded that although every day might not be a 10 out of 10 on the scale of entertainment, excitement, and fun, every day is a blessing, which makes it a good day. Let us do our best to speak life over our days. Let us not assume that just because a day might not be a mountaintop experience means that it will be a bad day. God Our Father is good every day!

If you have ever found yourself complaining about the average, mundane, and routine days, take the time to say this prayer. Heavenly Father, I just want to say "thank you." Thank you for all that you have done and all that you continue to do in my life. Thank you for my good days, and thank you for my challenging days. Thank you for my trials and thank you for my triumphs. Help me to remember to give you honor and glory every day of my life. Help me to be reminded of your blessings in even the smallest things in life. Help me to see and feel your love on the mountaintop and in the valley. I declare and decree that goodness and mercy shall follow me all of the days of my life. I speak your blessings over my life, and

I rejoice in this day that you have made. You are truly good, your mercy endures forever, and you are worthy to be praised every single day of my life. Forgive me of those times when I have taken your love and affection for granted. I love you and you are enough! In the name of Jesus, Amen!

REFLECT & RELATE NOTES

Lesson 21

"AUNTIE IS NEVER COMING OVER."

My daughter loves it when my best friend comes over. She rarely gets to see her because she lives out of state. It was the Thanksgiving holiday weekend and she was supposed to stop by our house at some point during the weekend. My daughter was aware that Auntie was in town, so she was eager to see her. We thought she would make it on Thanksgiving Day, but something came up. Each morning and throughout the day my child would ask, is Auntie coming today? Since I knew that my friend was in town for a specific purpose that weekend and was not certain which day she would be able to get over to our house, my response was "I am not sure, but she did promise to come over before she goes back home."

Friday passed, no Auntie, Saturday passed, no Auntie, and all day Sunday passed, and still no Auntie. After I had given my daughter her bath and was about to put her to bed on Sunday evening, she sighed and exclaimed, "Mommy, Auntie is never going to come over." I assured her that Auntie was going to come at some point before the end of the trip and not to lose hope. No sooner than I closed her door, our doorbell rang. Guess who was at the door? You guessed it, Auntie!

My daughter ran out of her room and zipped down the stairs to give Auntie a hug. They laughed and played with each other and my daughter even recruited Auntie to join me and her for the singing portion of her bedtime routine. Finally, Auntie had come and Nia was happy. This scenario so poignantly reminded me of times when I am waiting on the Heavenly Father to do something in my life. I know that He has promised me that He will do it, but He just does not seem to be moving as quickly as I think that He should be. Due to the Father operating on His schedule, I have found myself losing hope and thinking that "maybe He is not going to do it, maybe I heard Him wrong, and maybe I should just give up." Do these phrases ring a bell? Psalm 27:14 states, "Wait on the LORD: be of good courage, and He shall strengthen thine heart: wait, I say, on the LORD." Micah 7:7 states, "Therefore I will look unto the LORD; I will wait for the God of my salvation: my God will hear me." Psalm 130:5 states, I wait for the LORD, my soul doth wait, and in His word do I hope." Hebrews 11:1 also states, "Now faith is the substance of things hoped for, the evidence of things not seen." All of these passages are reminders that if our Heavenly Father said it, we can trust Him. It is so, and it will be done in His time. We must never lose hope, and we should keep the faith.

What have you been struggling to wait on God for? What areas have you found yourself starting to lose hope? Take some time to pray this prayer. Dear Heavenly Father, I first want to just thank you for being God. Thank you for being my father. Thank you for being true to your word. You are always on time when you show up and I thank you that I can always depend on you. Thank you that I do not have to lose hope. My faith is built on you and your word. Please forgive me for the times when I have struggled to believe and have started to lose hope. You have begun a good work in me and will perform it. I praise you for that. Please help me in the areas of _____

___ (fill in the blank with things you have been struggling to believe or have been losing faith about). I know that in due time, you will perform it. You operate on your timetable and not mine. I am confident that you know what is best. I praise you in advance for the victory. You are holy, you are worthy, and you are wonderful to me. In the name of Jesus, AMEN!

REFLECT & RELATE NOTES

_____

_____

_____

_____

_____

_____

_____

_____

_____

_____

_____

_____

_____

_____

_____

_____

Lesson 22

"IT ONLY MATTERS HOW I ACT AT SCHOOL. IT DOES NOT MATTER HOW I ACT AT HOME."

Now, let me tell you, God has blessed us to have an awesome student who tends to serve as a role model to peers at school and intently obeys what her teachers at school say. She does her work, zips those little lips when asked, and heeds the instructions outside of our home to the point of receiving awards at school for her stellar conduct. Nonetheless, the behaviors do not always transfer over at home. I might have to ask more than once for her to clean up her room or pick up her toys. I might have to remind her to watch her testy tone when responding to requests, or to answer me when I call her name. In the aforementioned moments, I remind my child that I know that she is very capable of doing what is requested, because she does what is asked of her all of the time at school, to the point where her teachers praise her conduct.

My little princess had just been awarded student of the quarter in her class. Shortly after the award, I tried to remind her that she might not get any more reward tickets (tickets students receive for behavior that can be redeemed for prizes) if she did not listen to what I had just asked her to do. Can you take a wild guess of what this child's response was? "It does not matter how I act at home. It only matters how I act at school."

My response to this was, "what you do at home is just as important if not even more important to what you do at school." Ahem... Does this sound at all familiar? Did you have to say "Amen," "Ouch," or both? These concepts reminded me to put the mirror up and evaluate my overall character, conduct, and obedience to my Heavenly Father at home and or when nobody else is watching. What we do at home is often even more important than what we do when others on the outside are watching, because our Heavenly Father always wants our obedience. He always wants us to heed His instructions even when no one else sees us. He always wants us to reflect Him. When we perform well at work, heed our supervisor's instructions, reply yes to every ministry opportunity that is presented, follow whatever the latest motivational speaker or guru says, but fail to follow what God says that is displeasing to the Father.

You may receive accolades for your work, a promotion on the job, and compliments on your latest performance review, but what is your spouse saying about you? What are your children saying about you? How are you treating your neighbors, or the waitress at the local restaurant? Is there unforgiveness in your heart? Do you use your social media to tear others down, or to build them up? He sees us in the public and in the privacy of our homes. Ephesians 4:1-4 states, "As a prisoner for the Lord, then, I urge you to live a life worthy of the calling you have received. Be completely humble and gentle; be patient, bearing with one another in love. Make every effort to keep the unity of the Spirit through the bond of peace." Psalm 19:4 states, "Let the words of my mouth, and the meditation of my heart, be acceptable in thy sight, O LORD, my strength, and my redeemer." God our Father wants us to live a holy, righteous, and acceptable life. Regarding obedience, Ephesians 6:1 says, "Children, obey your parents in the Lord: for this is right." The scripture does not just say to obey when we are at work, obey when others are watching, or obey at church, the Word says obey. Since God is our Heavenly Father, He wants us to listen to Him in any situation. God is not just asking this out of vanity and selfishness, He wants us to be a representation of Him wherever we go so that we might glorify Him and draw others closer to Him.

Are there areas in your home life or personal life that are not quite matching your outside life? Take a moment to pray this prayer. Father God, I want to thank you for allowing me the privilege to come to you in prayer. I praise you for loving me unconditionally. Right now I would like to ask for your forgiveness for all of the times that I disobey you. I am sorry for all the times that I do not follow the instructions that you have so plainly laid out through your word and the gentle nudging of the Holy Spirit. Please help me to forgive more, love more, and praise more. Let the character that I display in the world, match the character that I display at home. I want to be genuine and sincere in all that I say and do. Let my words, actions, thoughts, and feelings be acceptable and pleasing in your sight. I love and honor you. In the name of Jesus, Amen!

REFLECT & RELATE NOTES

_____

_____

_____

_____

_____

_____

_____

_____

_____

_____

_____

_____

_____

_____

_____

_____

Lesson 23

"BUT I DON'T WANT TO GO TO A NEW SCHOOL!"

We had sold our house, and as a result, we were moving to another home that was in another county. So you know what that means, yep you guessed it, a new school. I struggled with how to break the news to my precious child, as I knew how much she had enjoyed her first elementary school, nevertheless, the information had to be disclosed. As expected, the justified tears poured down her face and the sniffles were hard to bear listening to, nonetheless, the change had to take place. The last day of school was really the most difficult. When she got in the car, she was instantly reminded that this day would be her last day at a school she had called home where she had made wonderful friends and experienced an exciting kindergarten year with loving and nurturing teachers and staff. Nia did not understand why in the world this change had to take place.

She declared, "But, I don't want to go to a new school! I want to keep going to this school!" I tried to console her and let her know that I understood, but of course, at that very moment, there was not much that could be said to soothe her warranted sadness. After all, her current school was familiar. She had established roots there. The uncertainty of what to expect at a new school, and having to start all over making friends and getting acquainted with the new teachers and staff, was overwhelming. As my daughter struggled with this news, the word change came to mind. We all struggle with change. Whether it is the sudden loss of a job, severed relationship, or an unexpected grim diagnosis, change is hard! I would even go even further to say that the uncertainty that comes along with change is tough. We like to be in control. We like to know what is coming next and feel as if we are in control, but new circumstances can strip that sense of security.

A scripture that comes to mind when struggling in this area is Romans 8:28. Our Heavenly Father reminds us, "And we know that all things work together for good to them that love God, to them who are the called according to His purpose." I'll have you know that after my daughter went to her new school, discovered she had some friends there from our church and made new friends in the neighborhood; when I asked if she missed her old school and neighborhood, guess what she said, "NO!" She said she loved her new school, teacher, neighborhood, and house.

What change is happening in your life right now that is making you feel uncomfortable? What shift is looming that is producing feelings of fear and anxiety? Let us take this moment to pray over those areas. Dear God, my Father, thank you for reminding me that my life is in your hands. Please help me to embrace change and remember, that even though there are times that I do not understand what you are doing in my life, where you are taking me, why you are taking me there, and what is next, you are working all things together for my good. I place all of my anxiety, discomfort, and fear in your very capable hands, and thank you for giving me your peace, as I declare that I trust you with my life. You are a good Father and I praise your holy name. In the name of Jesus, Amen.

REFLECT & RELATE ACTIVITY: WORKED OUT FOR MY GOOD

"And we know that all things work together for good to them that love God, to them who are the called according to His purpose."

Romans 8:28

Situations that I stressed out about	Ways the situations worked out for my good

Lesson 24

"CAN'T I JUST GET WATER DUMPED ON MY HEAD?"

My child is quite the inquisitive one, and I am certain that I am not the only parent who can attest to this. She asks questions such as what does that word mean, how do you spell …, why do we do things that way, or how do you make this and that? One question that she sought the answer to was surrounding baptism. She said that she did believe in Jesus as her Lord and Savior but was a little apprehensive about baptism. She said she did not want to put her whole body into the water and was afraid of getting water in her nose.

117

The conversation then led to her asking, "Can't I just get water dumped on my head?" She went even further to ask if she could possibly just run through the water somehow. I must admit, I did internally snicker as I visualized her suggestions for baptism playing out in real-time, but I was able to maintain my composure and take the time to explain how baptism is carried out and the reason for it being carried out the way that it is. I explained the child appropriate answer that we get fully immersed in the water to symbolize dying to sin and being raised into a new life with Jesus. Nia was able to express understanding of the reason to get dipped all of the way into the water, although still slightly hesitant about going through the process. My daughter's questions for me made me think of James 1:5 that states, "If any of you lacks wisdom, you should ask God, who gives generously to all without finding fault, and it will be given to you." Just as our earthly children ask questions without hesitation to get understanding and meaning, we can ask our Heavenly Father questions. Our Father, God is always there to welcome us with open arms in our quest for wisdom. He can handle our questions about what, when, where, and how. He is ready, willing, and eager to shed insight into those areas that you are struggling to gain clarity.

Take a moment to think of areas in your life where you are seeking wisdom. Is there a decision you need help making but want to be sure that it is a wise choice? Is there an area that has been troubling you and you need your Heavenly Father's guidance on how to proceed?

Are you seeking meaning for your life and need God to reveal His will and plans for you? Let's take a moment to pray… My Father, my God, thank you for reminding me that I can seek wisdom from you. Thank you that you freely give wisdom when I lack understanding. Please help me to gain insight into _____ _____ as I have been struggling to understand, and after you give me the wisdom, help me to be able to apply and accept what you have said through our quiet time together and through your holy Word. I praise you because I know that you see all, hear, all, know all, and created all. You are truly worthy of all of my praise. In the name of Jesus, Amen!

REFLECT & RELATE NOTES

_____

_____

_____

_____

_____

_____

_____

_____

_____

_____

_____

_____

_____

_____

Lesson 25

"I DON'T LIKE BEING A BIG SISTER!"

For any child, and any person for that matter, change is hard. We all struggle to adjust from our once normal being shifted into something that would be classified as a new mode of operation. This is so true when my once only child became a big sister. You see, being a big sister is a blessing from the perspective that Nia had another child to play with, and a live baby doll to love on. Nonetheless, as Nia would put it, being a big sister has its drawbacks. Her little sister no longer was cute and cuddly when she started putting all of her toys in her mouth, or unknowingly/sometimes knowingly tore up her artwork, or made a mess in their playroom that

Nia had so meticulously just organized. Furthermore, having to share with Brielle who is not usually as willing to return the favor, or having to be a positive example, as she is older and should be a role model for appropriate behaviors, gets a bit weighty for a big sister.

Additionally, while the ultimate responsibility falls on parents, there is some responsibility that comes with being a big sister. On several occasions, my daughter has declared, "I don't like being a big sister." Now, I am well aware that my youngest knows just how to press her big sis's buttons. The lesson in their lives shows me what our Heavenly Father, God desires of us for our brothers and sisters in Christ, and even those who we want to come to know Christ. He wants us to be a positive example. Matthew 5:16 states, "Let your light so shine before men, that they may see your good works, and glorify your Father which is in heaven." God wants us to be loving even when others do not seem to be loveable. He wants us to be a light to those who may be new to the faith, or even those who do not appear to have any faith at all. He wants us to illuminate His character through forgiveness even when our brothers and sisters have wronged us. He wants us to be willing to share with our siblings (biological and spiritual), even when they are not willing to share with us. The ultimate goal for us to be the light is so that He can be glorified and so that others can come into the Kingdom of God by our living examples.

Take a moment to think about who God has placed in your life for you to be an example to. In what situations might you need to show more maturity so that your Heavenly Father can be glorified? Let us pray this prayer. Dear God, my Father, thank you for reminding me that I am your child. Thank you for all of the brothers and sisters that you have placed in my life, both biologically and spiritually. Please help me to love _____ _____ (fill in the names) the way you want me to love. Help me to give the way that you want me to give, and help me to forgive the way that you so graciously forgive me. Help me to be a living example for all with whom I come into contact so that others can come to know you as their Father too! You are so good to me and for that, I say thank you. In the name of Jesus, Amen.

REFLECT & RELATE NOTES

Lesson 26

"I'LL TAKE ONE OF EVERYTHING."

The Christmas season was upon us and that oh so strategic bullseye store mailed out the child mesmerizing holiday toy catalog. When my daughter laid eyes on the book, she was instantly captivated. She giddily and carefully browsed each page circling the items that she wanted for herself and her little sister. After Nia finished surfing the catalog, my husband and I asked which items she wanted for Christmas. Her response was, "I'll take one of everything," with a confident grin shining across her face.

Matthew 7:7 states, "Ask, and it shall be given you; seek, and ye shall find; knock, and it shall be opened unto you." My child had a bold request that she did not hesitate to share. Yes, she asked for ONE OF EVERYTHING! Now some may say, well that is a bit excessive, but my little girl did not think so. Of course, when Christmas morning arrived, one of EVERYTHING from the book was not under the tree, but many of her requests were. She also received a tent that she had not even verbalized wanting and admitted that she had really desired a tent. As a matter of fact, she revealed that the tent was her favorite of all the gifts.

I caught a glimpse of our Father that day. I saw that He loves to give us what we ask for. When we ask for one of everything, we might not get it all, but we also have to recognize our motives and make sure that we are not asking amiss as described in James 4:2-3. Our Father is ready to give us good gifts, we just have to ask. James 1:17 states, "Every good and perfect gift is from above, coming down from the Father of the Heavenly lights, who does not change like shifting shadows." Perhaps instead of scrolling through that toy catalog, you might be scrolling through the Bible and saying I want that peace that surpasses all understanding, I want that joy instead of sorrow, I want that abundant life that is available to me. You might also be saying, I want to be completely debt-free, house, car, student loan and all. I want to write that book, obtain that degree, or start that business. Petition your Father. He is listening. He said that you can ask.

Take a moment to think about what your bold ask for your Heavenly Father is today. Pray this prayer. Father God, thank you so much for being my Father who I can approach with my desires, hopes, and dreams. Thank you that I can trust you to meet all of my needs, and that I can believe that you desire to see my life prosper. I also want to thank you for those things that you did not give me because you knew that they were not the very best that you have in store for my life. Right now, I am boldly asking for _____ (fill in the blank). Your word says that I can ask and receive, seek, and find, knock, and the door will be opened, so right now I am asking, seeking, and knocking. Also, let my desires line up with what you want for me, as I do not want to be asking with the wrong motives or amiss. I only want what you want for me. You are truly the Father of every good and perfect gift. I praise you in advance for the many blessings to come, and thank you for all that you have already done. In the name of Jesus, Amen.

REFLECT & RELATE ACTIVITY: MY HOPES, DREAMS, AND DESIRES

Take a moment to list some of your hopes, dreams and desires that you can place in your Heavenly Father, God's hands.

Hopes

1. _____

2. _____

3. _____

Dreams

1. _____

2. _____

3. _____

Desires

1._____

2._____

3._____

Reflections

My brothers and sisters, as Part I comes to a close, did you see yourself or hear yourself saying some of the same phrases that my daughter stated? Were you able to draw nearer to Our Father, recognizing that you are His precious son or daughter? My prayer is that through Part I, you were able to catch a Glimpse of Our Father through my daughter's words and my response. I hope that you were reminded that you are His child. I hope that you were able to see that Our Father can handle your fears and frustrations. Our Father can heal your hurts and soothe your pains. Our Father just desires a personal relationship with you just as I desire a relationship with my child. He is ready and excited to hear your hopes, dreams, aspirations, and requests, and guess what, He does delight in answering your prayers. You just have to ask. As with earthly parents, because our Father loves us, He is not going to give us anything that we cannot handle or that is not beneficial for us, but as Psalm 84:11 states, "For the LORD God is a sun and shield: the LORD will give grace and glory: no good thing will he withhold from them that walk uprightly." He wants our obedience, patience, and contentment, so that we can live lives of peace and become all that He has created us to be. He wants to bless us, and we can talk to Him just like we talk to our earthly parents. We can trust Him to keep His word and always work ALL things out for our good! Even when we do not understand, even when we feel like we cannot trace Him, and even when we feel like He is not near, He is always available. He is ever present! He hears us when we call. He is our lifter and our healer. He is our encourager and our defender. He wants us to see ourselves the way that He sees us, which is holy, righteous, and very good because we are made in His image as the book of Genesis reminds us.

Let us pray. My Father, my God, thank you for reminding me that I am your child and you are my Father. I thank you for loving me unconditionally and that nothing can separate me from your love. Please open my eyes and prepare my heart to receive what else you have to say to me as I continue this journey of exploring more what parenthood reveals about your role as my Father. I love you and give you all of the praise. In the name of Jesus, Amen.

We will now continue our journey into getting more glimpses of God, Our Father as we explore words and phrases that I have said to my daughter, that I realize sound so much like what our Heavenly Father oftentimes tries to communicate with me as His child in Part II. Keep your pen handy and your hearts open to continue to receive more of what Our Father has to say as you continue this journey.

A PARENT'S PERSPECTIVE

How often do we get frustrated with God's instructions and corrections? There are times when we feel as if our Father is being punitive or unfairly strict, but that could not be further from the truth. Our Heavenly Father sees the bigger picture. After all, He is the creator of Heaven and Earth who knows all, sees all, has power overall, and is ever present with us. When God instructs us not to do something or hinders what we think should happen from happening, He is simply being the loving and protecting Father that He is. I am sorry to break it to you, but we are not the ones who are all-wise, all-powerful, and almighty, but guess what, our Father, God, is all of those things and more. Additionally, our Heavenly parent, God serves as an encourager, provider, leader, and guide.

Lesson 1

"DON'T TOUCH THAT HEATER."

Children are very curious, and you know what captures their attention the most? The very thing that we as parents tell them not to do. Now before you go saying, that is just what little people do, we know some grown-ups who are just as guilty. I see you ducking down and covering your face over there, but I am not judging you. I promise! Remember when God told Adam not to eat from the tree, but after Eve did, he partook? We all have a little Adam and Eve in us that can get us in trouble if we let it.

We have a portable heater in our family room because it can get a bit drafty. Even when the heater was not on and my daughter would attempt to play with it, I would tell her, "Don't touch that heater." One day, while the heater was on, she got very close to it and tried to touch it. Do you know what her response was? "Oh Momma, that is HOT." I did not have to say, "I told you so" to my daughter because she was able to see for herself, but why is it in our nature to do the very thing(s) our Heavenly Father, God tells us not to do?

Why do we sometimes have to get burned or experience intense heat, pressure, or pain before we heed the instruction or warning that our Father has given us? The apostle Paul had it right in Romans 7:15-20, "I do not understand what I do. For what I want to do I do not do, but what I hate I do. And if I do what I do not want to do, I agree that the law is good. As it is, it is no longer I who do it, but it is sin living in me. I know that good itself does not dwell in me, that is, in my sinful nature. For I have the desire to do what is good, but I cannot carry it out. I do not do the good I want to do, but the evil I do not want to do—this I keep on doing. Now if I do what I do not want to do, it is no longer I who do it, but it is sin living in me that does it."

Instead of having to try things out for ourselves and ending up battered, bewildered, or bruised let's live on the Word of our Heavenly Father that says, "Submit yourselves, then, to God. Resist the devil, and He will flee from you," James 4:7. We can also remember that our Father says in 1 Corinthians 10:13, "No temptation has overtaken you except what is common to mankind. And God is faithful; He will not let you be tempted beyond what you can bear. But when you are tempted, He will also provide a way out so that you can endure it."

What are some areas in your life that have been your greatest temptations? What areas do you need to ask the Father to help you no longer indulge in? He is waiting with open arms to help. Pray this prayer. Father, God, I know that you love me and that you can deliver me from all of my temptations. I ask for your courage, strength, and wisdom to flee from _____ (fill in your answers from above) so that I might please you and have all that you have in store for me. I am tired of being burned, bruised, and hurt. I know that you know best. You have plans to prosper me and not to harm me. You hear me when I call. So I am calling out to you for help. Heal, deliver, and set me free. Thank you in advance for the victory and the same overcoming power that raised Jesus from the dead. In the Name of Jesus, Amen!

REFLECT & RELATE NOTES

Lesson 2

"SLOW DOWN SO THAT YOU DON'T FALL."

My daughter had just learned how to walk and as she began to gain confidence in walking, she would start to run. Sometimes she would run so fast that she would not notice that she needed to slow down until she mastered walking. Secondly, she did not notice any obstacles in the way such as a toy she had left on the floor, or the concrete beneath her that could cause unnecessary scrapes and bruises if she fell. She would also try to run ahead of me and my husband, but we would tell her to slow down so she could remain in our sight so that we could ensure her safety.

I was reminded that we do the same thing to our Heavenly Father. We try to run ahead of Him, not realizing that we need to slow down. Whether it is jumping into marriage before knowing enough about the person we are dating, to making impulsive and or rash financial decisions that could have long-term negative consequences, we try to run ahead of God rather than slowing down. Sometimes we want what we want when we want it. We are moving so fast that we don't realize we may fall flat on our faces, and bruise, break, or destroy something. Proverbs 21:5 states, "The plans of the diligent lead to profit as surely as haste leads to poverty." Translation, slow down! Take your time! Remember that this life is meant to be a marathon and not a sprint. We do not want to be assistants in our own lack or loss. We want our God our Father to be our pacesetter and guide so that we can profit and succeed.

Take a moment to examine the areas in your life that you may be rushing ahead of God. Which areas do you need to be still and know that He is God? What areas do you need to let the Heavenly Father take control and help you pace yourself? Pray this prayer. Dear Heavenly Father, thank you for being with me. Please forgive me for the times that I try to run ahead of your plan, purpose, and will for my life. Help me to slow down and rest confidently knowing that you are here to help me every step of the way. You are all-powerful, all-knowing, and ever-present. You are the ultimate pacesetter for my life, and for all of these things, I say thank you. Right

now I am turning over _____
(fill in your answers from above) to you, and I look to
you as my guide. Thank you for being patient with me
as I trust, lean, and depend on you. In the name of Jesus,
Amen!

REFLECT & RELATE NOTES

Lesson 3

"Help me clean up."

Anyone who has ever had a toddler running around in the house knows it is close to impossible to keep a clean house 24/7. My daughter will have books, puzzle pieces, crayons, dolls, paper, the list goes on and on, dispersed all over the place. Now, do you think I helped her put all of these items here, there, and everywhere? Of course not! Nevertheless, instead of cleaning up for her, as I would do at times, the older she got, the more I elicited her help in cleaning up her mess. I purchased some pretty pink and purple storage bins and began to show her how to place her toys in the bins when she was finished playing with them. After showing her, she got better and better with cleaning up by me telling her to do it.

The same is true with us as God's children. We often make messes in our lives. We could have chosen to go our own way, disobey His instructions, or fall into the various traps of destruction that the enemy has set for us. Whatever the mess is that we find ourselves in, God is always there willing to clean us up, but we do have to help Him. Help means that we do have to change our ways and turn from those things, and He has His hands extended in our direction with an unwavering willingness to help. We do have to do our part, however. Sometimes we think that we should just be miraculously delivered from our messes. While this is very possible, because there is nothing impossible with Him, this is not always the route Our Father takes with us. There is some effort required on our part. Yes, I said E-F-F-O-R-T and HARD WORK!

We don't typically get into messes overnight, therefore the clean-up process does not occur overnight. One prime example of a mess that we as adults tend to create is debt. You might say that you want to get out of debt and be more financially responsible. While a million-dollar check could just show up in your mailbox tomorrow morning *(sounds nice, right, come on through Lord!)* typically that does not happen. The actions needed would be staying out of the mall, getting off of that one click shopping website, cutting those credit cards up, creating a budget (and sticking to it), and living within your means. James 2:17 states that "In the same way, faith by itself, if it is not accompanied by action, is dead."

What messes exist in your life that came to mind as you read this page today? Get those examples in mind and pray this prayer. Heavenly Father, I thank you for always being with me. Thank you for helping me clean my life up. Thank you for reminding me that you can make all things new in my life and you have the power to create in me a clean heart. You have the power to renew my spirit. You have the power to deliver me out of pits and out of the hand of the enemy. Thank you for being an ever-present help in a time of trouble. You are an awesome Father and I praise you that even though I disobey your voice and prompting at times, you are always there with open arms to not only accept me but to help me clean up. Please give me the strength to go through this cleanup process and continue to remind me that you have never and will never leave me because nothing can separate me from your love. Also, please forgive me for all of the times I created unnecessary messes. Thank you for your unfailing love. In the name of Jesus, Amen.

REFLECT & RELATE ACTIVITY: CLEAN-UP TIME

Areas of my life that are a bit "messy":

1._____

2._____

3._____

Steps that I can take to begin the cleanup process with the help of my Heavenly Father:

1._____

2._____

3._____

Lesson 4

"STOP EATING THAT PAPER, EATING THAT LINT, DRINKING YOUR BATHWATER (OLD DIRT) WHEN I AM TRYING TO WASH YOU CLEAN OF THOSE THINGS."

Bath time is such a fun time in our house. My daughter loves to play with her bath toys accompanied by lots of bubbles. There are times however when my daughter decides that it is a fabulous idea to drink her bath water and try to eat the soap that is formed by the bubbles. I find myself having to remind her that it is not healthy for her to drink her bathwater and soap. There was also that phase where she liked to put everything in her mouth and eat things that are not meant to be edible such as lint and paper. Once again, I had to remind her not to eat those items either. While in her eyes it may seem like I am being a mean parent who does not know what I am talking about, I am actually instructing her in a way that has her best interest, health, and wellbeing in mind.

How many times does God have to tell us to stop doing things that are harmful to us? How many times do we return to old ways, thoughts, or behaviors? How many times do we view our Heavenly Father's instruction, Word, and guidance as a nuisance or as punishment? How many times do we think that we know better or our way is a better option? We may not see the harm in these things, but He does because He sees all, knows all, and is all powerful. He wants nothing but the very best for us as His children. As Psalm 32:8 states, "I will instruct thee and teach thee in the way which thou shalt go: I will guide thee with mine eye."

Our Heavenly parent, God, is always there to lead, guide, and direct us, and we can trust His directions. The Word also states that "The thief cometh not, but for to steal, and to kill, and to destroy: I am come that they might have life, and that they might have *it* more abundantly" John 10:10. God wants us to have a full life, so anything that He is telling us not to do is something that would detract from the abundant life that His word speaks of.

What have you been "consuming" that you need the Father to help you let go of? What dirty things in life have you been holding on to or trying to keep taking in that the Father has already washed away from your life via the precious blood of Jesus? Take this time to pray this prayer. God, my Father, thank you for washing me clean through the blood of Jesus. Thank you for wanting what is best for me and having awesome plans for me. Thank you that you want me to have an abundant life. Please forgive me for consuming _____(fill in the blank of people, places, and things that come to mind) that are not good for me when you have already cleansed and set me free from those things. You are wonderful, you are mighty, and you are good. In the name of Jesus, Amen.

REFLECT & RELATE NOTES

_____

_____

_____

_____

_____

_____

_____

_____

_____

_____

_____

_____

_____

_____

Lesson 5

"EAT YOUR FOOD SO THAT YOU CAN BECOME BIG AND STRONG."

There are certain vegetables my daughter does not like to eat. While some veggies are not the tastiest to the pallet, we as parents know the importance and nutritional value of broccoli and those vitamin-filled carrots. Along the lines of eating, one of my daughter's favorite phrases is "I'm hungry." When she said she was hungry, we quickly figured out that she might not have been hungry, but rather that was our cue that she wanted a treat of some sort. Candy, cookies, snacks, you know, all of the tasty delights that having too much of could be a negative thing—she wanted those foods.

We would have to encourage her to eat her dinner first and eat a certain amount of her vegetables before having the snack or treat that she really wanted when she said that she was hungry. As with natural food, our role as God's children is to feast on His word as it brings nutrition and value to our spiritual bodies. When we do partake in God's word, we also have to have a well-balanced plate. We cannot just have the scriptures that talk about prosperity without reading the scriptures that talk about patience. We cannot just have the passages that talk about victory without having to read the scriptures about going through trials. We have to not only have the words that encourage and strengthen us without also having the words that correct and prune us. How often do you study the word? An even better question is, how balanced is your word diet?

John 6:35 reminds us that "Jesus declared, I am the bread of life. Whoever comes to me will never go hungry, and whoever believes in me will never be thirsty." Matthew 4:4 also reminds us, "But He answered and said, "It is written: 'Man shall not live by bread alone, but by every word that proceedeth out of the mouth of God." We have to live by and feast on EVERY word in the Bible. That means we cannot just pick and choose which portion of our Father's words to consume. ALL of the words that God provides through the scriptures are there to satisfy our soul's hunger and quench our spiritual thirst.

Take a moment to examine your spiritual diet and then pray this prayer. Dear Father God, thank you for your word. Thank you that "All scripture is given by inspiration of God, and is profitable for doctrine, for reproof, for correction, for instruction in righteousness: That the man of God may be perfect, thoroughly furnished unto all good works" as 2 Timothy 3:16-17 states. Thank you for reminding me to study your word in its entirety. Help me to have a balanced plate and diet as I feast on your word. Please continue to lead, guide, and direct my path. Order my steps in your word so that I might become all that you desire for me to be. I want to be healthy and strong in you so that I may give you glory through all that I say and all that I do. I also want to rightly divide your word of truth. Please give me clarity and revelation as I study. I love your word and appreciate that you gave me free access to your voice by way of the Holy Bible. You are worthy of all of my praise. In the name of Jesus, Amen.

REFLECT & RELATE ACTIVITY: MY SPIRITUAL PLATE

Identify areas of your life that you need direction, strength, and wisdom so that you can be healthy and strong spiritually (ex. peace, forgiveness, joy, love). On the plate below, put the topic and a corresponding scripture passage that you can feast on for the week. Feel free to repeat this activity as often as needed.

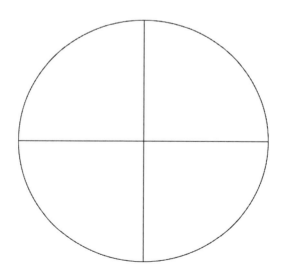

Lesson 6

"YOU CAN COME OUT OF THE TIMEOUT."

My daughter loves to be the sous chef in the kitchen with my husband and me. Whether it is scrambling the eggs, putting cheese on the pizza, or putting seasoning in a pan, she enjoys pitching in. We enjoy having her company. Nevertheless, there are times when we have her step aside, particularly around the stove due to the heat. One day, she decided she wanted to help pour the salt in the skillet. I told her that she could not and that I would need to do it. Rather than heeding my instructions, she proceeded to attempt to pour the salt in. In the process, she dropped the entire salt canister into the pan, causing much of the salt to spill out.

Before I could even form her name on my lips, she put her head down, stepped down from her stool, and picked her stool up. Upon picking up her stool, my child disappeared from the kitchen as I continued to cook. When I got to a stopping point, I proceeded to find Nia. I discovered that she had gone to the bathroom. My precious child had closed the door and was sitting on the stool with her head hanging down. My little one had placed herself in timeout. She was looking so pitiful yet extremely adorable at the same time. She knew what she had done and was truly sorry for it. My heart melted because I saw the remorse and regret in her eyes. I talked with her in a calm voice and said, "you can stay in timeout for a few more minutes, but when you come out, you can continue helping me." I was not at all angry at her, and the fact that she was truly sorry made all of the difference.

Are you catching a glimpse of our loving heavenly parent, God? What God wants from us is a repentant heart. How many times do we do wrong, sin, and have to sit ourselves down with the recognition that what we did was wrong? Just as I felt compassion for my daughter and still loved her despite her mistake, I wanted her to come back and help me. God wants us to confess our sins and know that He is faithful and just to forgive us of all of our sins, and cleanse us of all unrighteousness as is stated in 1 John 1:9. There is no condemnation in Christ (Romans 8:1), so we do not have to hold ourselves hostage to our mistakes. If He forgives us, surely we should forgive ourselves.

What mistakes have you made that you still find yourself hanging your head down in shame? Are there matters from your past that you feel make you unworthy to be in the presence of or of service to our Heavenly Father? Get those answers in mind and pray this prayer. Heavenly Father, thank you for being such a forgiving God. Thank you also for conviction, because I know that conviction leads to the correction of my behaviors and sins. Right now, I confess and turn from _____ _____ (fill in the blank). I am so very grateful for your forgiveness and unfailing love. Help me release myself from guilt, shame, and condemnation, as I know those are not of you. You are a God of love, joy, peace, longsuffering, gentleness, goodness, faith, meekness, and temperance as Galatians 5:22-23 reminds me. I cannot say thank you enough for all that you have done. You are great and greatly to be praised. In the name of Jesus, Amen.

REFLECT & RELATE NOTES

_____

_____

_____

_____

_____

_____

_____

_____

_____

_____

_____

_____

_____

_____

_____

Lesson 7

"I AM SO PROUD OF YOU!"

There have been several times when I have been proud of my daughter. Whether it was the very first time that she crawled, the time that she took her very first step, or the time she cleaned up all of her toys on her own, I was proud of her. Whether it was the time that she shared her Easter eggs with the little boys at the park who did not get as many at the local Easter egg hunt, put on her pants for the first time, or whether it was her simply following directions, I was proud of my child. The list goes on and on of times I have said and or thought this about my child. Each time I verbalize these words, she lights up like a Christmas tree, and in many instances repeats the actions. Did you know that our Heavenly Father, God is the same way with us?

161

While our works do not save us or make God love us any more or any less, our obedience is what He desires. He is pleased when we walk in His will and His way. He is pleased when we are a positive reflection of Him. The Word reminds us in 2 Peter 1:17 "He received honor and glory from God the Father when the voice came to Him from the Majestic Glory, saying, "This is my Son, whom I love; with Him, I am well pleased."

Just as I am proud and well pleased when my daughter is obedient, God is proud when we obey His Word, follow His instructions, and listen to that still small voice that 1 Kings 19:12 refers to. He is pleased when you let that driver get in front of you in the middle of rush hour traffic, when you take care of your sick loved one when other family members will not, when you serve in that ministry without any recognition, or when you are kind to that not so loveable coworker or customer. He is pleased when you forgive, even when it is difficult, when you say "yes" to your calling, even when others might not see it yet, and when you do your work as unto the Lord, even when you might have got passed over for that promotion. Our Father, God is proud of you!

Take a moment to reflect on your life. What actions or behaviors have you demonstrated that is a reflection of your Heavenly Father for which you know He is proud? Pray this prayer. Father God, thank you for reminding me that You are proud of me. I give you all the glory and honor for giving me the ability to do _____
_____ (fill in the blank). I

desire to live a life that honors you and brings glory to your name. You are my creator and you are my Father. I want others to see your reflection in me so that they can come to know you more. You are truly an amazing Father. Please help me to continue to please you with all that I say and all that I do. As Psalm 19:14 states, "Let the words of my mouth, and the meditation of my heart, be acceptable in thy sight, O LORD, my strength, and my redeemer." In the name of Jesus, Amen.

REFLECT & RELATE NOTES

_____

_____

_____

_____

_____

_____

_____

_____

_____

_____

_____

_____

_____

_____

Lesson 8

"TONIGHT, YOU HAVE TO GO STRAIGHT TO BED; NO STORYTIME, NO PLAYING GAMES, JUST PRAYER, AND BEDTIME."

When my husband and I say this to our daughter, oftentimes it is a consequence of her not doing something that she was supposed to do. While the nightly routine always includes taking a bath and saying prayers, other fun stuff like sight words, piggyback rides, jumping on the bed, and singing is what gets excluded when we have to tell our daughter that she has to go straight to bed. One day, we received a report from school that she had not listened to her teacher and as a result, had to go into a timeout. This is an example of one of the nights that she had to go straight to bed.

Did our love change for her just because she had gotten in trouble? No. Did we want to disown her as our daughter? Of course not. Did we think any less of her because of her actions? Absolutely not! This is true for us as God's children. There are times when there are consequences for our disobedience. We might experience sickness due to poor food choices, experience heartbreak because we decided not to listen when the Father said that he or she was not the one, or experience calls from the creditors because we decided to use credit to purchase items that we could not afford. Nevertheless, the Father still loves us. He has not forgotten us. He has not abandoned us, and He does not see us any differently. HIS LOVE IS UNCONDITIONAL!

Part of unconditional love is discipline though. Our sin does yield consequences yet does not take away God's love. The Bible reminds us of this in Hebrews 12:4-11 which states, "In your struggle against sin, you have not yet resisted to the point of shedding your blood." And have you completely forgotten this word of encouragement that addresses you as a father addresses His son? It says, "My son, do not make light of the Lord's discipline, and do not lose heart when He rebukes you, because the Lord disciplines the one He loves, and He chastens everyone He accepts as His son." Endure hardship as discipline; God is treating you as His children. For what children are not disciplined by their father? If you are not disciplined—and everyone undergoes discipline— then you are not legitimate, not true sons and daughters at all. Moreover, we have all had human fathers who disciplined us and we respected them for it. How much more should we submit to the Father of spirits and live! They disciplined us for a little while as they thought best; but God disciplines us for our good, so that we may share in His holiness. No discipline seems pleasant at the time, but painful. Later on, however, it produces a harvest of righteousness and peace for those who have been trained by it." That passage was packed with goodness, but I will summarize it. Our Father loves us, but in His love, He must discipline us when we are disobedient. Discipline should however not be despised but embraced because it is confirmation that our Heavenly Parent, God, loves us and is trying to mold us into the best version of ourselves.

Has the enemy tried to trick you into believing that just because you have experienced consequences that the Father does not love you? We cast down that thought right now in the mighty name of Jesus! You are undoubtedly loved by your Heavenly Father, God! Pray this prayer. Thank you Father God for reminding me through your word that you discipline me because you love me. Thank you that you proved your love for me over 2000 years ago at the cross by sending your only Son to cover all of my sins even before I committed them. You are amazing. Please forgive me of _____ (fill in the blank) so that I might be cleansed of all unrighteousness. I want to please you. I praise you for your unconditional love and for your correction. You are an awesome Father. In the name of Jesus, Amen.

Reflect & Relate Notes

Lesson 9

"LET ME HELP YOU."

As many of you know, three-year-olds can strive to be very independent. Once they think they have learned a skill, they do not want any help. I was working with my daughter on brushing her teeth, but she tried to take the toothbrush away so that she could brush her teeth on her own. She had not quite mastered brushing all of her teeth as the toothbrush went back and forth on her two to four front teeth only. I had to pry the toothbrush out of her little hands to assist with brushing the remainder of her teeth. You know, the side teeth, molars, and do not forget her tongue. After all, neglecting to brush all of her teeth could result in cavities, bad breath, and overall unhealthy dental hygiene.

Another skill she was fascinated to learn and that she thought she had mastered was putting on her shoes. While she had the concept of putting both feet in her shoes, her left shoe was on her right foot and her right shoe was on her left foot. The shoes looked good to her but remaining in shoes on the wrong feet could get uncomfortable over time. While I admire her tenacity and zeal for attempting newly acquired skills, evidence suggested that the skills were not yet mastered and required additional assistance from Mommy. How many times do we try to do things on our own without the help of our Father, God? God may have given us a glimpse of His plans for us or allowed us to explore a new venture but we try to execute the tasks and activities on our own. We fail to realize that we have not yet mastered the skills and need our Father's help.

How often is the Father saying, "let me help you," and we ignore His voice resulting in unnecessary abrasions, blemishes, and bruises because we did not simply heed His voice? Psalm 121:2 states "My help *cometh* from the LORD, which made heaven and earth." Also, Proverbs 3:5-6 reminds us to "Trust in the LORD with all thine heart; and lean not unto thine own understanding. In all thy ways acknowledge Him, and He shall direct thy path." We all need God's help, as we cannot live, move, and have our being successfully without Him. After all, He desires to assist us. You are His and He is yours.

What have you been trying to do on your own that you have not been allowing our Father, God, to help you with? Get those areas in mind and pray this prayer. Father God, thank you that my help comes from you. Thank you for reminding me that you are the vine and I am merely a branch that can do nothing apart from you. Thank you for reminding me that in you I live, move, and have my being. Please order my steps, guide me, and lead me because I want to be in your will. I need your help. Right now, I commit _____ (fill in the blank people, places, circumstances) to you. I know you are the all-wise God so right now I give control back to you. Please forgive me for the times when I forget to seek you and try to do things on my own or prematurely. I love you and thank you for hearing my prayers. You are truly a good Father. In the name of Jesus, Amen!

REFLECT & RELATE NOTES

_____

_____

_____

_____

_____

_____

_____

_____

_____

_____

_____

_____

_____

_____

_____

Lesson 10

"YOU CAN DO IT. DO NOT BE AFRAID."

There are two times a year that our church distributes speeches for the youth to memorize and recite for a special holiday program. You guessed it, Christmas and Easter. Each time my husband and I work with our daughter to learn her speech so that she can learn something new about her Heavenly Father, God, and share that message with our church family. She does an excellent job of learning her speech and saying it with confidence at home. She would practice with her flashlight as the microphone and boldly proclaim her speech. She even proudly recited her speech to her grandparents, or as we call them, GG and Paw Paw, and had even turned her speech into a song.

175

As I drove her to rehearse her speech at church, I even heard her whispering her speech in the back seat of the car. When she got on stage to practice the speech that she had learned three weeks in advance, the day she received the speech, guess what came out of her mouth? Nothing. NOT....A....Word...! My amazing and once confident little one just stood there as if she had no idea what her speech was. She was paralyzed by fear. The speech coordinator encouraged her to speak, but she refused. The director invited me on the stage to assist, but my child just clung to my leg and refused to speak. As I knelt at her side, and reminded her that she knew her speech and that she could do it, she firmly squeezed my leg and uttered "auh, auh, I don't want to say my speech."

I tried to remind her not to be afraid and that she could do it, but she would not share her speech. The coordinator interjected again and suggested Nia stand with a partner to deliver her speech, but she still refused. We prayed and figured that by the next day, the day of the program, she would minister her speech. We tried bribery. Hey, don't judge me! I know I am not the only one. We told her that she could have one of her favorite pieces of candy if she said her speech. She then told us she would be willing to recite her speech with a friend by her side. Upon arriving at church, we connected with one of the other little girls and she agreed to share the stage with my daughter. I told my daughter I was proud of her and that "Daddy and I will be on the front row cheering you on."

So, speech time rolled around. My daughter and her friend graced the stage, her friend said her speech, and my little one even confidently took the microphone. My husband and I smiled, gave her a thumbs-up, and mouthed that she could do it. We thought she was going to open her mouth, but instead remained silent. No speech. She knew it, but all we got was crickets. After a few moments of waiting, the audience proceeded to clap, and my daughter and her friend exited the stage. This reminded me of the scripture passages that I had shared with my child prior to her speech. Philippians 4:13 states, "I can do all things through Christ which strengtheneth me," and 2 Timothy 1:7 states, "For God hath not given us the spirit of fear; but of power, and of love, and of a sound mind." Isaiah 41:10 states, "Fear thou not; for I am with thee: be not dismayed; for I am thy God: I will strengthen thee; yea, I will help thee; yea, I will uphold thee with the right hand of my righteousness."

I had hoped that by sharing the passages she would find comfort and be able to say her speech. We were there for her; she could see us. She knew what to do, and we knew that she was fully capable of performing, nevertheless, she struggled. The same can be true for us as God's children. How often do we let fear paralyze us and prevent us from pursuing goals, visions, and dreams that God has prepared us to accomplish? How often do we freeze on the stage of life when we have been called to speak the truth that we know because we are afraid? We must remember that our Father, God, is there just as my husband and I were for our daughter. He is cheering you on, telling you that you can do it, and reminding you that He is there every step of the way. What you have to say is important! This sometimes dark and evil world needs YOUR words, talents, and gifts so that they too can see the love of our Heavenly Father whom we continue to talk about in this very book.

In what areas do you find yourself being paralyzed by fear? What is something that you know the Father has equipped and prepared you to do, but you have not stepped out to "perform" due to fear or doubt? Take a moment to pray this prayer. Dear Heavenly Father, thank you for reminding me that you have not given me the spirit of fear. Thank you for reminding me that I CAN do all things through Christ. Thank you for reminding me that you will NEVER leave me nor forsake me. YOU ARE WITH ME. Thank you for reminding me that if you, God, are for me, then who can be against me? Thank you for reminding me that I am more than a conqueror through Christ Jesus. Please help remove the spirit of fear in the areas of _____ _ (fill in the blank). Help my confidence to be in you and all that you can do through me in these areas. You gave me the spirit of power, love, and a sound mind, so help me to walk in those qualities so that the world can hear you, see you, and feel you through me. I love you, thank you, and trust you. In the name of Jesus, Amen.

REFLECT & RELATE NOTES

_____

_____

_____

_____

_____

_____

_____

_____

_____

_____

_____

_____

_____

_____

_____

_____

Lesson 11

"I KNEW YOU COULD DO IT!"

Every two years, our family is blessed to have a family reunion. One of the traditions of our reunion is to have a talent show during our banquet. Any family member of any age can sign up to participate in the talent show. We always look forward to seeing who has a talent and who might not need to quit their day job. Now I know that is not just my family that has that one cousin who just knows they are going to be the next singing competition winner. Anyhow, to my surprise, when Nia heard about the talent show, she excitedly proclaimed that she wanted to participate. When I inquired as to which talent she would like to display, she replied, "I want to sing in the talent show."

Was this the same child who would not utter a single word on the stage for her Christmas and Easter speeches? Was this the same little one that I had to bribe to speak, and she kept her lips sealed? I knew she could do it but was a bit surprised that she volunteered to perform by herself in front of all of our family. After the fleeting moment of surprise passed by, I began to go into preparation mode. I asked her what she was going to sing and what she was going to wear. Because we had not brought any attire that she thought was stage ready, we went and purchased a cute little rainbow-colored skirt to go with the pink shirt that she already had. She chose to accessorize with her sunglasses, and Poppy headphones (including bright pink Poppy hair for all my *Trolls* watchers). Just before showtime, we went to the dressing room, aka, the venue bathroom, to make final preparations. It was at that point Nia began to express nervousness and doubt that she would actually sing. I reminded her again, that I would be right there, and that she could do it.

After enjoying several family members display their talents, and deep belly laughing at others, it was Nia's turn. The DJ did not have her song, so she opted to sing acapella. With headphones on, sunglasses secured, and her stylish outfit neatly adorning her figure, with the microphone in hand Nia nervously began to SING! We heard "When Jesus say yes, nobody can say no…." The selection by Michelle Williams proceeded from my child's mouth. As she sang, we cheered, and guess what? She sang the whole song. Upon completion, she was greeted with cheers, "Good job", and "We knew that you could do it!" I share this story as a part b to the "You can do it, don't be afraid" section of the book because it is important to remember the times that we perform, act, move, speak or proceed even when we are afraid.

Even when anxiety, doubt, and nervousness try to block our performances, we can push through anyway. As I was there cheering my child on with confidence that she could sing in front of our entire family, so is God, our Father looking down from Heaven cheering us on. He always reminds us that we can do all things through Him as Philippians 4:13 states. Also, we can rest in the fact that if God is for us who can be against us. We are more than conquerors through Him as Romans 8:31 and 37 highlights. We have no reason to fear or let anxiety and fear paralyze us because God is with us as Isaiah 41:10 so beautifully declares.

When was a time that you did something despite experiencing fear? Write those situations down and write down the feelings you experienced as a result of moving forward despite anxiety, fear, or nervousness. Now let us pray. Father God, I just want to thank you for all of the times that you helped me do things when I felt afraid. Thank you for reminding me that I can do all things through you. Thank you for always being with me and equipping me with everything that I need to move forward in every area and path that you have ordained for me to walk through and partake in. You are an amazing and never-failing Father. In the name of Jesus, Amen.

REFLECT & RELATE ACTIVITY: FACING MY FEAR

A situation I acted on despite anxiety, fear, or nervousness	Reasons I was fearful	How did I conquer the fears?	How did I feel after pressing forward despite fear?

Lesson 12

"YOU CANNOT WATCH THE 'VIRAL VIDEO' WEBSITE ANYMORE."

I must admit that there were times that I would let my daughter watch, yes, you guessed it, YouTube. She had mastered finding videos that piqued her interest. In the beginning, my husband and I were very conscious of what she was watching and monitored the videos she viewed. After all, the "viral video" website did allow her to learn her ABCs at a very young age. As time progressed, she became more and more fascinated with the app and would view various, what appeared to be child-friendly videos. My husband and I became more lax on monitoring the videos she watched. There would

185

be times, however, we would see or hear something in one of her videos that we would say, "no, you need to find another video, we do not like that one." She would proceed to change it.

Still, there were times when I might have been preparing dinner, or doing something else, that I permitted her to watch her tablet. I noticed towards the end of her threes, she started to get an attitude that I did not recognize and struggled to follow directions. She was whining more than usual and not listening as much as she used to. I began to ask her where she got those behaviors from. Who had been modeling that behavior because I knew that was not happening at home or daycare? I concluded that there had to be some of these behaviors being displayed on some of the videos she had been watching. In the midst of one of her tantrums of opposition, I declared, "You cannot watch YouTube anymore!"

I can still picture that day as clearly as if it just happened yesterday. My husband and daughter were in her room about to go through the bedtime routine, I had asked her to do something, and she replied with a smart remark, and then I said it. "You cannot watch YouTube anymore." Neither my husband nor I were ready to hear what was about to come out of our toddler's (going on teenager) mouth. She boldly stated "I'm weeeeaving (leaving)" and proceeded to walk out of her room into the hallway! Trying with all of our might to hold in our laughs and maintain stern facial expressions, we asked,

"Well, where are you going?" Her response was, "I don't know."

I then explained that the reason we were taking the application away was because we had noticed some uncharacteristic behaviors and attitudes that were likely picked up by watching some of the videos. My words seemed to go in one ear and out of the other. She continued to misbehave and I then stated again, "You are not going to be able to watch the YouTube anymore." For a second time, my teenage toddler made the same declaration that she was "weeeeaving" and proceeded to walk out of her room again. We gave her alternatives. We told her that while she could no longer watch YouTube, she could continue to view her educational programs and spend more time with activities such as games and outdoor play. Besides, where in the world was she going to go? Her grandparents still laugh about this as they jokingly stated that they would leave the porch light on for her. Mind you, they live hundreds of miles away. She had no plan. For a brief moment, she thought leaving would solve her problem, when in reality, all we were doing was looking out for her best interests and desired conduct that was becoming of our dear child.

How often do we decide we want to turn from Our Father, God when He takes things from us that we thought were perfectly fine for us to have? How often do we start off doing things that seem harmless but end with us acting in unbecoming ways? It could be engaging in relationships with toxic people, holding conversations that turn sarcastic, listening to music that has a good beat, but derogatory lyrics, or even as my daughter was doing, watching inappropriate programs on TV or the internet. The issues may seem subtle and as if they are not impacting our views, character, or actions, but the more we are exposed to those unhealthy people, situations, programs, or places, the more we start to imitate the same inappropriate behaviors.

Our Father wants us to look like Him and reflect Him in all that we say and all that we do. Genesis 1:27 reminds us that "So God created man in His *own* image, in the image of God created He Him; male and female created He them." He also deposited into us the fruit of the spirit: "But the fruit of the Spirit is love, joy, peace, longsuffering, gentleness, goodness, faith, meekness, temperance: against such there is no law," found in Galatians 5:22-23.

In the process of our Heavenly Father making us look like Him, sometimes He has to remove some people, places, and things that do not look like Him. This process can be hard because we think we are missing out on something. Our Heavenly parent, God, sometimes removes jobs, relationships, and circumstances that we would have otherwise remained in because we thought we were comfortable and did not realize that we were not being good reflections of Him. Do not lose hope in that though. The awesome news is that He still gives us healthy and holy alternatives. As we gave our daughter the option to continue to watch her tablet as long as she was watching educational videos, playing games, coloring, doing puzzles, or participating in outdoor play, God does the same for us. He can replace all of those toxic areas with better jobs, healthier relationships, and other circumstances that promote positive growth and ultimately bring glory to His name. Additionally, let's not be so quick to flee or as my little one put it "weeeeve" situations where, let's just say our Pastors, best friends, bosses, or spouses are providing constructive feedback and speaking the truth in love regarding our actions, but we are being too stubborn or hardheaded to receive the correction.

What is it that you need to allow Father God to cut out of your life or modify so that you can look more like Him? Instead of turning from Him thinking that He has forsaken you or thinking He is mad at you, take a moment to pray this prayer. God, my Father, I first want to thank you. Thank you for creating me in your image. Thank you for equipping me with the fruit of the Spirit. I would like to ask that you forgive me for all of those times that my attitudes and actions do not represent you. Also, please forgive me for all of the times that I have not received correction and feedback that was only given to help me become all that you have called and ordained me to be. Help me to stop running from situations that are only trying to make me more like you. Please reveal areas where I need to change or remove that are hindering me from being a shining reflection of you. I want people to see you when they see me. I praise you for your unconditional love, for hearing my prayer, and for always forgiving me no matter how many times I fall short. You are good, and I give you all of the glory. In the name of Jesus, Amen.

REFLECT & RELATE NOTES

Lesson 13

"It's bath time."

Seven-thirty. That is the time I habitually run my daughter's bathwater. After running the water, putting her bath toys in the tub, getting her toothbrush ready, preparing her towels, and getting her pajamas out, I faithfully shout from the top of the stairs, "Nia's it's bath time." Many days she would come running up the stairs eager and ready to take her bath. There are exceptions to those days though. If she is highly engaged in a coloring activity, watching one of her favorite TV show, or is just flat out trying to avoid going to bed because she wants to stay up that night, she will reply back "but I do not want to take a bath" never mind the fact that she had a busy sweaty day at school and had been playing outside at the park on a very hot and humid day. Now, how does taking a bath relate to us as God's children, you might be thinking? I'm glad that you asked.

Many times, we get dirty with the issues of life and the sins of this world. Dirty with a bad attitude because of something we just saw on the news, dirty with an evil tongue because that person just cut us off in traffic, dirty with selfishness because we think that because we worked hard to obtain a certain status and we are unwilling to share our knowledge and resources with others because we don't think that they are deserving. I could continue because I know that the list goes on and on, but I will allow you to take a moment to fill in the blank to make it personal. We are so busy being occupied with our sins and or comfortable in those sins that we don't want to allow our Father, God to wash us clean of those things. We may even go as far as say, "but that is just the way that I am, and I am not changing," yet He is steadily calling us to come so that He can wash us, bathe us, clean us up, and make us new, but we resist. Psalm 51:7 says, "Cleanse me with hyssop, and I will be clean; wash me, and I will be whiter than snow." We need our Father to clean us up. That is part of His nature as our Father!

What areas of your life do you need the Heavenly Father to cleanse? My hope is that you even include those areas that seem like they have permanently stained you, and those areas where you say "well that is just the way that I am." He can wash you clean of those too! Take a moment to reflect and then pray this prayer. Dear God, my Father, thank you for being the ultimate cleaner. Mr. Clean has nothing on you, Father God. Thank you for washing my sins away day after day. Thank you for allowing your only Son, Jesus' blood to be shed so that I might be made clean. Right now, I confess _____ (fill in the blank). Please cleanse me, create in me a clean heart, and renew a right spirit within me so that I can be more like you. I love you with all of my heart and want to please you with my life. In the name of Jesus, Amen.

REFLECT & RELATE NOTES

Lesson 14

"I HEARD WHAT YOU SAID, AND I DID NOT FORGET."

Most parents can relate to our children repeating questions or statements over and over until they hear us respond. There are even times that we do respond right away, but they continue to repeat their questions, requests, or statements. My daughter will even ask the question, "Mommy, are you listening to me?" While I must admit, as a natural parent, it can get slightly annoying to hear the same question over, and over, and over, and did I say over again, our Heavenly Father is not like that? Praise the Lord!! Thank Ya Jesus!! He does not get annoyed by us. He is not bothered by our requests. He is listening and He hears us every time. Psalm 116:1 states, "I love the Lord, because he hath heard my voice and my supplications." Our God welcomes our requests and petitions. 1 John 5:14-15 states, "And this is the confidence that we have in Him, that, if we ask anything according to His will, He heareth us: And if we know that He hear us, whatsoever we ask, we know that we have the petitions that we desired of Him." A thought to consider with our Father hearing our prayers is that although He hears us, that does not mean that He answers right away. Also, His answer might not be what *we* think it should be. His answer could be yes, no, or wait. We have to learn how to be content and patient with whatever response we receive. We can be confident and comforted in knowing that regardless of His answer, He loves us, He hears us, and He has our best interests in mind.

What questions have you been asking your Heavenly Father that you have been thinking are falling on deaf ears? What prayers have seemed to be receiving the silent treatment or as if they are not being heard? What have you even heard the Father say yes to but also coupled that yes with a "wait?" Take this time to pray this prayer. Heavenly Father, thank you for reminding me through your word that you do hear my prayers. Thank you that I can come boldly to you. Thank you that your ears are attuned to what I say. Thank you that although you might not operate on my timetable or as quickly as I think you should respond, you are always right on time. Thank you for the yeses, no's, and the waits, because you do know what is best. Please help me to continue to trust you and remember that just as I hear my children when they call, you hear me, your child when I call. I love you Father. In the name of Jesus, Amen!

REFLECT & RELATE ACTIVITY: MY PRAYER REQUESTS

"And this is the confidence that we have in Him, that, if we ask anything according to His will, He heareth us: And if we know that He hear us, whatsoever we ask, we know that we have the petitions that we desired of Him."
1 John 5:14-15

Make a list of your current prayer requests. I also encourage you to highlight, circle, or put a checkmark by the requests when you see your Heavenly Father answer your prayer.

1._____

2._____

3._____

4._____

5._____

Lesson 15

"YOU CAN GO TO PRIVATE PRE-K."

I have always been a planner when it comes to children (and other areas for that matter). When my husband and I got married, we said we wanted to wait 4-5 years before having our first child. Five years into our marriage, I was pregnant with our daughter. I then said that I did not want to have to pay for two children to be in childcare at the same time, so the plan was to have our second child once our first was able to enroll in state-funded pre-k. So guess what, God blessed us to get pregnant while my daughter was three, and by the time she would be four, our second baby would be born. We applied for public pre-k and my daughter was accepted. Awesome, right? Everything had gone how we planned. Wrong.

Our first daughter had been attending an in-home Christian daycare from the time she was around five months and would remain there until it was time for pre-k. Mrs. D had done such a phenomenal job not only teaching her about the Lord, but also prepared her immensely for school. Nia was already able to recite sight words, write letters, count to 100, and count by tens. You get my point. When my husband and I attended the orientation for the public pre-k program and remained after the meeting to talk with the provider about the curriculum, we found that our child already knew that information. With that being said, we began to explore the curriculum for private pre-k. We wanted our daughter to be challenged. We did not want to stunt her growth. We wanted her to continue to excel academically, so you already know what decision we made. The two of us unwaveringly decided to pay for private pre-k. While the cost would require some sacrifices and self-denial on our part, our child was worth it. Her future was worth it. We wanted to give her the best because we love her and want her to succeed. Now, by no means am I bashing the public program, because there is value in the program and it is a great opportunity to engage in any early learning initiative. I am saying that there are other options as well that may be a better fit for each individual child and his or her current academic level, so thankfully, with God's help, we were able to enroll her in the class that met her where she was.

Another interesting point to note surrounding enrolment in the pre-k school was that the school we decided to enroll her in was the very same school that we would pass on the way to Mrs. D's that she would always say, "Momma, I want to go to that school one day." There are multiple glimpses of God in this situation. God, our Father does the same for us. He wants the very best for us, sacrificed for us, and paid the cost so that we could receive the critical gift of salvation and eternal life. The word tells us that God gave His only son as a sacrifice for us because He loved us that much, and with Jesus being the ultimate sacrifice for us by laying down His life, He came that we might have life and have it more abundantly as is referenced in John 10:10. Also, Jeremiah 29:11 reminds us "For I know the plans I have for you, declares the LORD, plans to prosper you and not to harm you, plans to give you hope and a future." By Nia getting to go to the school that she had unknowingly prophetically been asking to go to, she asked and received, knocked, and the door was open as Matthew 7:7-8 states.

Are there any areas of your life that come to mind where you are settling for less than the best? What are the areas where good is being the enemy to great in your life? Your Heavenly Father wants to do more. Can you also think of any time your Heavenly Father has done more than you had imagined? When is a time that you asked and received, sought, and found, knocked, and the door was open? Get the answers to the previous questions in

mind and pray this prayer. Dear Father God, thank you for having my best interest in mind. Thank you for all that you have already done. I praise you for _____
_____ (fill in the blank of abundant blessings and answered prayers). I also praise you in advance for what is to come. Please forgive me for all of the times that I doubt you or settle for less than the best that you have in store for me. I love and praise your holy name. In the name of Jesus, Amen!

REFLECT & RELATE ACTIVITY: EXCEEDING AND ABUNDANT BLESSINGS CHART

"Now unto Him that is able to do exceedingly abundantly above all that we ask or think, according to the power that worketh in us."
Ephesians 3:20

Heavenly Father, thank you for already blessing me with the following that was beyond what I could ever ask or imagine could be possible:

1._____

2._____

3._____

4._____

5._____

Lesson 16

"YOU JUST HAD YOUR 4ᵀᴴ BIRTHDAY."

When my daughter had her 4th birthday, she would proudly go around telling people that she was four. If someone asked her how she was doing, she would say, "I am four," with a priceless grin on her face. Days into "fourhood," she started announcing, "I am going to be five." Of note, my child reaching four was already an emotional motherly moment, as I reflected upon how fast the first four years of her life passed by. Now, she was already trying to rush through age four to get to age five. My response to her stating that she was going to be five was, "Nia, you just had your 4th birthday. Let's take some time to get used to being four and enjoying that age." I reminded her that she would eventually be five, but another year would need to pass first. She proceeded to share "yeah, 5, then 6, then 7, then 8, then 9, and then 10." Well, at least we know she can count, right?

Anyhow, my daughter's plight to be five years old just days after her fourth birthday reminded me of times in our lives when God has blessed us to reach a goal or milestone. We earned that high grade we wanted, we graduated, we landed the job, we were selected for the promotion, we purchased that new home, we received healing from sickness, etc..., yet instead of focusing on the victory and the present stage or state that we are in, we are already looking for the next lesson, page, or phase in our lives. While it is okay to dream and look forward to the future, we must not be so busy focusing on the future that we miss recognizing the beauty and gift of the present. In the present, we should take the time to reflect on the goodness of our Heavenly Father and all that He has already done for us. Matthew 6:34 states, "Therefore do not worry about tomorrow, for tomorrow will worry about itself. Each day has enough trouble of its own."

Have you found yourself forgetting to enjoy today? Have you been worried about your future? What victory, milestone, or new gift do you need to spend more time focusing on and praising your Heavenly Father for? Take time to pray this prayer. Heavenly Father, thank you for this season of my life. Thank you for your many blessings and victories. Right now I give you glory for __ _____ (list your gifts, milestones, accomplishments). You are truly worthy of all the glory and all of the praise. When I find myself focusing too much on the future and forgetting to remain in and reflect on the present, please redirect my focus and forgive me. I love you. In the name of Jesus, Amen.

REFLECT & RELATE NOTES

_____

_____

_____

_____

_____

_____

_____

_____

_____

_____

_____

_____

_____

_____

Lesson 17

"I'M SO SORRY BABY GIRL, I KNOW IT HURTS."

I am from the old school when it comes to taking my children out post-birth. My mother taught me to wait until my babies got their shots at 6-8 weeks before taking them out in the world. The reason for this is to protect them from sickness and disease, as their immune systems are fragile at such a young age. Despite knowing the benefits of the shots, it was still very painful for me to hold my daughter's arms as the nurse pricked her little legs three times with the much-needed vaccinations. I cringed and apologized for the pain as my daughter cried out after each prick. As soon as the nurse finished administering the shots, I picked my whimpering baby girl up to console her, held her close, let her know that I loved her, and let her know that I was there. I apologized and let her know that I knew those mean ole shots hurt!

This experience reminded me of how our Heavenly Father is with us when we experience uncomfortable and or downright painful experiences that are ultimately working out for our good. Romans 8:28 comes to mind that states, "And we know that in all things God works for the good of those who love Him, who have been called according to His purpose." Once again, this passage is a friendly reminder that no matter how painful, uncomfortable, or challenging situations get, our God, our Father WILL work everything out for our good! I must admit that the more I meditate on that passage in my own life, the more peace and comfort manifest within me and I hope that the same is true for you too.

What life circumstances seem to be so painful that there seems to be no way that the situation can, has, or will work out for your good? I challenge you to give those circumstances to God and find comfort and confidence in His word that IT IS WORKING FOR YOUR GOOD! Pray this prayer. Father God, thank you that you have always worked things together for my good. Even when things do not make sense to me, even when it hurts, even when I feel confused, I want to find comfort in knowing that you are working ALL things out for me. I thank you for my trials, and I thank you for my victories because today I choose to do as your word states to give thanks in everything. You are the perfect creator and fixer of all things, and for that, I give you glory. In the name of Jesus, Amen.

REFLECT & RELATE NOTES

_____

_____

_____

_____

_____

_____

_____

_____

_____

_____

_____

_____

_____

_____

_____

_____

Lesson 18

"YOU ARE FEARFULLY AND WONDERFULLY MADE. YOU ARE A CHILD OF GOD. HE LOVES YOU, AND THAT IS ENOUGH!"

This is the declaration I taught my daughter, particularly after hearing people were treating her unkindly at school. I wanted her to know who she is and whose she is without a shadow of a doubt. I know that if she knows who she is, no matter what challenging people or circumstances come her way, she will be better equipped to handle whatever comes her way. This is the same wish that our Heavenly Father has for us. He wants us to meditate on His word as Joshua 1:8 states, "This book of the law shall not depart out of thy mouth; but thou shalt meditate therein day and night, that thou mayest observe to do according to all that is written therein: for then thou shalt make thy way prosperous, and then thou shalt have good success." The first portion of Proverbs 23:7 also reminds us, "For as He thinketh in His heart, so is He."

There is power in our thought life, and power in what we feed our minds. Trials will come. The enemy will try to test and trick us into believing we are less than the blessed, holy, prosperous, righteous, royal, and successful people that we are. He will try to make us think we are inferior, but guess what? That is a lie. The enemy is the father of lies, author of confusion and his only desire is to steal, kill, and destroy us. By studying who our Heavenly Father says we are, we can conquer obstacles and we become all that He has destined and created us to be despite what others may say. The more that we study His word, the more we will believe what He has to say about us instead of believing the lies of the enemy.

What challenges have you had in life that have tried to trick you into thinking less of yourself than your Heavenly Father says about you? What negative thoughts have you been meditating on as opposed to positive truths that your Heavenly Father freely spells out in His Word? Take the time now to write down challenges to those negative thoughts with the words of our Father, God, and begin to declare those words over your life. Pray this prayer. Father God, thank you for reminding me that I am fearfully and wonderfully made. Thank you for telling me that I am made in your image and likeness and I am good because you are good. Thank you for loving me unconditionally and that being enough. Thank you that I am a royal priesthood and a holy nation, and a chosen generation. You are good and worthy to be praised. Thank you so much for being such a loving Father who I can always come to for comfort and always know that my worth is found in you because I am your child. In the name of Jesus, Amen.

REFLECT & RELATE ACTIVITY: THOUGHT CHALLENGE CHART

Negative Thought/Lies from the enemy	What God Says About Me and or My Situation

Lesson 19

"I LOVE YOU."

The most common times I tell my daughter that I love her is right before I leave her room at night and when I drop her off at school in the morning. No matter what has happened during the day, I love my daughter. Even if we had a rough night leading up to bedtime, I love my daughter. Even if she has been disobedient, I love her. Even if she is sick and vomits all over me, I love her. Even if she has gotten in trouble, I love her. Even when I think about times when she was an infant with stinky poo poo diapers, guess what? I love her.

As I mentioned earlier, I tell my child that I love her when I drop her off at school. My hope is that she remembers this when challenges present, and they will at some point during the day at school. I want her to remember that if someone is unkind to her, Mommy loves her. If she does not understand something that is being taught, I love her. If she is having a great day, I love her, and if she does not know what to do, I love her. I also want her to have my love on her mind because I cannot always be physically present with her. Is this starting to hit home about our Heavenly Father's love for us? He LOVES us. He LOVES YOU! NO MATTER WHAT.

Romans 8:35-39 states, "Who shall separate us from the love of Christ? Shall tribulation, or distress, or persecution, or famine, or nakedness, or peril, or sword? As it is written, for thy sake we are killed all the day long; we are accounted as sheep for the slaughter. Nay, in all these things we are more than conquerors through Him that loved us. For I am persuaded, that neither death, nor life, nor angels, nor principalities, nor powers, nor things present, nor things to come, nor height, nor depth, nor any other creature, shall be able to separate us from the love of God, which is in Christ Jesus our Lord." The passage clearly can be translated to say that NOT ONE person, place, or thing can get in the way of our Heavenly parent, God's love for us as His children. Now that is what is called agape love. Whew, thank you God! Hallelujah! What a blessing, right?!

Have you been thinking that our Father does not love you? Have you ever felt separated from His love? Have you done something that you have thought, "He cannot possibly love me after I did _____ (fill in the blank)?" Well, I am happy to report that you have been tricked by the enemy. GOD LOVES YOU! Your Heavenly Father not only loves you, but He also wants YOU to love you. Take this time to pray this prayer. Dear God, my Father, thank you for loving me unconditionally. Thank you for not only forgiving me of my sins, but as Micah 7:19 states, "You will again have compassion on us; You will tread our sins underfoot and hurl all our iniquities into the depths of the sea." Thank you for not only forgiving me and not letting anything separate me from your love, but not holding my flaws or sins against me. Wow, what a love! Help me to love me when the enemy tries to make me think that I am unlovable. Please continue to remind me that your love is unconditional. I thank you, love you, and glorify you for your grace and mercy. You are truly worthy to be praised. In the name of Jesus, Amen!

REFLECT & RELATE NOTES

_____

_____

_____

_____

_____

_____

_____

_____

_____

_____

_____

_____

_____

_____

Lesson 20

"PLEASE BE STILL."

I often find myself asking Nia to be still. Whether I am washing her hair or styling it on a day to day basis, "please be still" proceeds out of my mouth. While trying to complete the hairstyling task, my daughter frequently states, "Are you done yet" or "Momma, please hurry up?" I tend to tell her that if she would just be still a little while longer, the task will be complete and she can be free to move about or return to doing something she would much rather be doing. Additionally, she will be able to see the finished product of a beautifully styled crown of glory. After all, she finds joy running to the mirror once her hair is freshly done and stating how "pretty my hair is Momma!" During the process, however, I also have to let her know that the more she keeps moving, the longer the styling process is going to take. The Word of our Heavenly Father states, "Be still, and know that I am God; I will be exalted among the nations, I will be exalted in the earth." Psalm 46:10. Busyness can sometimes be counterproductive to our progress, although our natural thinking oftentimes depicts the opposite. Psalm 46:10 reminds us, however, that there are times that we just need to stay put so that our Father, God can do the work on our behalf.

What situations come to mind in which you find yourself moving around? In what circumstances are you having trouble just being still so that your Heavenly Father can work? Take a moment and pray this prayer. Father God, thank you that your word gives me comfort in knowing that I can be still and know that you are God. In knowing that you are God, thank you for further reminding me that you are working, you are moving, and I will see victory in my life because you are my Father. Thank you for also reminding me that Philippians 1:6 states, "Being confident of this, that He who began a good work in you will carry it on to completion until the day of Christ Jesus." Please help me to wait on you. Help me to know that you are God. You are working all things out for my good, and I will see your salvation in the land of the living. I trust you. I love you. I praise you. I can confidently be still knowing that you have all power in your hands. Thank you for being such an awesome Father. In the name of Jesus, Amen.

Reflect & Relate Notes

_____

_____

_____

_____

_____

_____

_____

_____

_____

_____

_____

_____

_____

_____

_____

_____

Lesson 21

"IF YOUR DADDY SAID IT, THEN IT IS TRUE."

We were planning to go out to breakfast with one of the ministries that we were part of, and children could attend. My daughter ALWAYS gets excited about going out to eat. My husband had told her that we would be going to MiMi's. The night before the breakfast outing, my daughter approached me and asked "Mommy, are we going to MiMi's?" I then fired back with a question of, "Who said that we were going to MiMi's?" She retorted, "Daddy said it." I then responded, "Well if your Daddy said it, then it is true."

When we tell our child that we are going to do something, we do our very best to follow through, so she can be confident in what we say. Even more importantly, our Heavenly Father is perfect (unlike us) and cannot lie. Numbers 23:19 states, "God is not a man, that He should lie; neither the son of man, that He should repent: hath He said, and shall He not do it? or hath He spoken, and shall He not make it good?" While we, as parents, might occasionally not keep our word even with the best of intentions, our Heavenly parent, God ALWAYS keeps His Word. If He said it, IT WILL BE DONE! Can I get an Amen?!

What is something you keep questioning that you know, that you know, that you know, that your Father, God, has promised? If you are having a hard time being confident that it (whatever IT is, you fill in the blank) will be done, take a look over your life and jot down all of the promises your Heavenly Father has kept. Take a moment to pray this prayer. Father God, thank you for truly being a man of your word. Thank you for being the truth and for being so reliable. Help me to cast my worries and doubts on you and replace them with hope and faith that you will do just what you said. I praise and glorify your wonderful name. In the name of Jesus, Amen!

REFLECT & RELATE ACTIVITY: PROMISES KEPT

"God is not a man that He should lie; neither the son of man that He should repent: hath He said, and shall He not do it? or hath He spoken, and shall He not make it good?"
Numbers 23:19

5 Promises that God has Kept

1._____

2._____

3._____

4._____

5._____

Lesson 22

"WE ARE NOT GOING TO FLY THIS TIME. WE WILL BE DRIVING."

For the Thanksgiving holiday, we usually travel to New York to celebrate. For the first few years of my daughter's life, we would fly. As the Thanksgiving holiday approached, Nia expressed excitement that we would be getting on a plane to New York. She commenced disclosing how much she enjoyed flying on an airplane. I sadly had to burst her bubble that this year…we would not be flying. You see, this was the first year that we would have to purchase an additional ticket for our younger daughter Brielle, as she was now over the age of 2. To be cost-effective, we would need to drive instead.

Well, let me tell you, the news of having to spend 14 hours in the car, not be able to take that fantastic voyage to the airport, and not be able to board that thrilling airplane just zapped the joy out of my young one, and she burst into tears exclaiming sheer disappointment that she would not be getting to New York by the method she most preferred. Fast forward, once the time came for the trip, my child's excitement returned because she realized where she was going, the fact that she was going with her parents and sister, and the fact that she was going to get to see her family, especially her cousins. She did not even seem phased by the fact that we were driving.

My child handled the ride both going and returning home in a stellar manner. Nia did not merely endure the ride, she enjoyed the journey once she accepted the path and mode for the trip. This reminds me of times when we are used to our Heavenly Father showing up one way or in a certain amount of time, but He chooses another method or mode, that may sometimes be longer than we expect. When we learn to submit to His will and His timing for our lives, everything seems to smooth out and even become enjoyable. Proverbs 16:9 reminds us, "In their hearts humans plan their course, but the LORD establishes their steps." We can have a plan of how we think things should go in our lives, but ultimately, our Heavenly Father has the final say of if, how, where, and when those plans will come to fruition.

Is there something in your life that you know God has shown you will take place, but the route seems too long or the mode by which the Lord is seeking to transport you seems unappealing? Take a moment to get that situation or circumstance in your mind and pray this prayer. Dear Father, thank you for knowing what is best for me. Thank you for ordering every one of my steps. Thank you for reminding me that you know what is best and which way that I should go. Please help me to not just endure my journey but rather enjoy each moment of my life because I know that I can trust you in everything. No matter how far, long, or unfamiliar the route, help me to remain confident that you are the driver, you are the pilot, you are the captain, and with you in control, I can be confident that I will arrive where you want me to be when you want me to be there. Thank you, Lord, for being a trustworthy and dependable Father! In the name of Jesus…Amen!

REFLECT & RELATE NOTES

Lesson 23

"LET'S TRY CHANGING WHAT YOU KEEP THINKING ABOUT."

N ia had let my husband and I know, quite early, that she was not much of a fan of watching movies because she believed she would get scared if she watched. Nevertheless, one evening, I figured that the two of us would have a movie night and watch a movie that reminded me of my childhood. I decided that we could watch *The Little Mermaid*. After all, I did not find the movie scary. *The Little Mermaid* was the first movie that I remember going to the theater to see with my mother. Furthermore, that movie was so dear to my heart, because I remember acting in a play at my elementary school as one of four Ariels (my drama teacher wanted to share the wealth for the leading roles). I even briefed my child with all of this information before watching the movie. She was not very impressed but reluctantly agreed to watch the film.

I won't give the play by play of her experience watching the movie, but it is what happened after that is worth highlighting. As I tucked her in that evening, she told me that she was having trouble falling asleep because she kept thinking about the evil octopus, Ursula, and her evil eel crew. She shared how scary she found them. She kept telling me that she just could not get that part of the movie out of her head. I took the time to gently validate her feelings and share how I know how those characters were super scary, but I also encouraged her to try to change what she kept thinking about. Instead of focusing on the evil octopus, perhaps we could try focusing on how the story ended, and that in the end, Ariel triumphed over that wicked Ursula. She struggled with shifting her thoughts. I tried asking what were some of the good parts of the movie that she could think of, but that did not work either. Lastly, I suggested she think of her favorite praise and worship songs that we sing at bedtime, and to sing those songs to herself to try to shift her attention. She tried that for a moment. That tactic worked briefly, but then she admitted that the scary parts of the movie just kept creeping back into her mind. Her feelings were real, and I bet that sounds familiar to you too.

Philippians 4:8 reminds us, "Finally, brethren, whatsoever things are true, whatsoever things are honest, whatsoever things are just, whatsoever things are pure, whatsoever things are lovely, whatsoever things are of good report; if there be any virtue, and if there be any praise, think on these things." When we find ourselves struggling with fear, anxiety, doubt, or any other troubling emotions, our Heavenly Father, God, encourages us to meditate on honest, just, pure, and lovely thoughts. He goes on to remind us to focus on things that are of a good report, virtuous, and praiseworthy. He knows that life brings on circumstances that could potentially lead us to fret, and the enemy tries to snatch the Word of God out of our minds when we are most vulnerable so that we struggle, but we do not have to. We can indeed think about what we are thinking about, and shift our thoughts to what our Father says that we should be thinking so that we can have His peace that surpasses all understanding.

Take a moment to think about areas in your life that you need to shift your focus. What is keeping you up at night in an attempt to steal your sleep and your peace? I encourage you to first give those concerns to your Heavenly Father and then shift your thoughts. I do recognize that thought shifting can be quite challenging, but with the help of our Heavenly Father, it can be done. Let's pray this prayer. Dear God, my Father, thank you for giving me a remedy to address all of these thoughts that keep troubling me. Right now I turn over my concerns surrounding _____ (fill in the blank). I declare and I decree at this moment that I will think about those things that you encourage. Help me to remember that because I have you, I win, no matter what things might look like right now. Please fill me with your peace that surpasses all understanding as I submit this prayer to you. I praise you in advance for renewing my mind daily and delivering me from these thoughts that keep trying to steal my joy. You are good, and I give you all of the glory, honor, and praise. In the name of Jesus, Amen! Now take a moment to complete the chart. Prayerfully this will help you in your thought shifting journey. Feel free to make copies of this page for yourself to complete as needed.

REFLECT & RELATE ACTIVITY: I CHOOSE TO THINK ON THESE THINGS

"Finally, brethren, whatsoever things are true, whatsoever things are honest, whatsoever things are just, whatsoever things are pure, whatsoever things are lovely, whatsoever things are of good report; if there be any virtue, and if there be any praise, think on these things."

Philippians 4:8

What is true?	
What is honest?	
What is just?	
What is pure?	
What is lovely?	
What is of good report?	
What is virtuous?	
What is praiseworthy?	

Lesson 24

"PLEASE STOP COMPLAINING."

Whether she is telling us she does not want to clean up after her little sister, is bored because we don't have any activities planned outside of the house for the day, or she is bored because we are just going to take a ride around town, oh how the complaints flow. Sometimes a full meal has been prepared but she says she would rather eat at McDonald's, or she would rather use the tablet instead of the iPad, the complaints get into full effect. During those moments, I find myself getting a bit frustrated and having to tell my child to "Please stop complaining."

I try to remind her that there are so many positive happenings in her life and so many blessings, yet the complaints continue. I remind her to take a little time to enjoy the ride as there is so much beautiful scenery that God created that can be admired, and remind her that she should be thankful for the food that was prepared for her, as there are so many people in this world that are going hungry and wondering where their next meal is going to come from. I share the fact that some do not even have any electronic devices, so the fact that she has a choice of which one to use, is something worth gratitude rather than complaints. Furthermore, I remind her that having a little sister to play with, share toys with, and sometimes have to clean up after is also a gift, as there are lonely children in the world who wish they had the company and toys that she has. Still, the complaints do not seem to cease. Are any of these sounding familiar?

My daughter's grumbling oftentimes makes me take a pause and look at my own patterns of murmuring and ingratitude. While our adult complaints might not relate to toys, devices, meal options, or cleaning up after our siblings, we do travel down the entangling path of complaining from time to time and need to be reminded to stop complaining. Our Heavenly Father has been too good for us to dwell in complain-land. Philippians 2:14-15 reminds us, "Do everything without grumbling or arguing, so that you may become blameless and pure, "children of God without fault in a warped and crooked generation." Then you will shine among them like stars in the sky." For further convincing that we should shift from a complaining spirit, Numbers 11:1 states, "Now when the people complained, it displeased the LORD; for the LORD heard it, and His anger was aroused. So the fire of the LORD burned among them, and consumed some in the outskirts of the camp." Woah! That sounds like God is not a fan of our complaining, AT ALL. Now I know that life does get tough, circumstances do not always go our way, we may not be where we want to be or have what we think we should have within certain timeframes and seasons in our lives, but complaining is not the remedy for our infirmity.

"Well what is the answer?" you might be asking. I am so glad that you did! Contentment, gratitude, praise, rejoicing, and thanksgiving are the answers. Philippians 4:11-12 states, "I am not saying this because I am in need, for I have learned to be content whatever the circumstances. I know what it is to be in need, and I know what it is to have plenty. I have learned the secret of being content in any and every situation, whether well fed or hungry, whether living in plenty or in want." In this passage, Paul does use the words "learned to be content." This means it is a learning process that we just might not get overnight, but with practice, we too can learn to be content.

Another helpful passage to aid in this process of contentment and not complaining is found in Psalm 34:1 which states, "I will bless the LORD at all times: His praise shall continually be in my mouth." Instead of taking a complaint break, take a praise break! I could go on and on with passages that show us how to give thanks, be grateful, and bless the Lord at all times, but in the interest of time, I will press the pause button right here. I do, however, have an assignment for you... when you find yourself getting into complaint mode, stop, check yourself, and begin to read scriptures on praise, thanksgiving, blessing, gratitude, and contentment. Then make a list of everything that you can be thankful for. Feel free to repeat this activity as those sneaky tendencies of grumbling and murmuring do resurface from time to time. Watch how much better you feel when your thoughts and language shift to praise and thanksgiving.

Now let us pray. Father God, I love you. I adore you. I praise you. You are truly worthy of all of my worship. Please forgive me for murmuring, grumbling, and complaining. Instead of counting what I do not have, who I am not with, or where I have not gone, let me count my blessings. You are good and have been exceedingly and abundantly good to me. Help me to remember all of your blessings and promises so that this lethal spirit of complaining can dissipate. I want to thank you for never giving up on me and continuing to extend your grace and mercy. You are truly an amazing Father. In the name of Jesus, Amen.

Reflect & Relate Activity: My Chart of Gratitude and Thanksgiving

"In everything give thanks: for this is the will of God in Christ Jesus concerning you."
1 Thessalonians 5:18

Instead of complaining, Father God, I am grateful and want to thank you for…

_____

_____

_____

_____

_____

_____

_____

_____

A Glimpse Of Our Father

_____

_____

_____

_____

_____

_____

_____

_____

_____

_____

_____

_____

_____

_____

_____

_____

_____

_____

Lesson 25

"WHY DO I HAVE TO KEEP REPEATING MYSELF?"

I find myself both pondering and verbalizing to my child "Why do I have to keep repeating myself?" I may have asked her to make sure that she places her dirty clothes in her hamper, yet her garments remain on her bedroom floor, or encouraged her to remember to flush every time, however, this slips her mind, and the toilet had an unpleasant surprise. On one occasion when I had given a directive, she belted out, "but Mommy, sometimes I do not understand what it is that you are asking me to do." Other times, Nia informs me that she is sorry, but she just forgot. In other instances, I know that she is flat out ignoring my instructions because she may be preoccupied with playing with her toys, using the tablet, watching TV, or she outright does not want to do what is being asked of her.

Regardless of the reason for me having to sound like a broken record, the question that I frequently find myself asking my child led me to make a connection with what our Heavenly Father must think when He gives us directions, commands, guidance, and instructions through His Word, and we fail to respond. The reason for our lack of responsiveness can vary. As with my daughter, we sometimes don't have full clarity of what is being asked, we are distracted, or we are clear, but are just being stubborn to follow His Word. Whatever the reason, as I try to be with my child (notice I said TRY with the help of the Lord-inserts smiley face and praying hands), to be patient. I am so thankful that our Heavenly Father, God is patient with us. As Psalms 86:15 states, "But you, Lord, are a compassionate and gracious God, slow to anger, abounding in love and faithfulness." He is patient with us and gives us time to get it right. Whew, thank you Lord! Over and over again, He repeats directives throughout His Word. He tells us to love our enemies, but we sometimes get even instead. He tells us to forgive, but we hold on to grudges. He tells us that our body is the temple of the Holy Spirit, but we put any and everything into our bodies. I know that I am driving down somebody's street right now. God does love us enough to repeat Himself because He wants us to be all that He has created us to be, and for that, I have to take a moment to say "HALLELUJAH!"

Take a moment to examine times where you know that you have ignored what your Father, God has asked of you. Also, examine any areas in your life where you think He may be instructing you in, but you are in need of clarity. Take a moment to pray this prayer. My Father and my God, I want to first thank you for your patience. Thank you for never giving up on me despite the times when I get distracted or even ignore your directions. I am so grateful that You pursue me over and over again and that your love for me is never-ending. Right now I ask that you forgive me for not heeding your guidance and commandments in the areas of _____ _____ (fill in the blank). Please give me the strength to listen to your promptings the first time. I love you with everything that is within me and give you all the praise, and I thank you for loving me unconditionally. I ask all of these things in the name of Jesus, Amen.

REFLECT & RELATE NOTES

Lesson 26

"CELEBRATE WITH YOUR SISTER."

My younger daughter's birthday was approaching and my older daughter was eager to give input on birthday gift ideas. A host of suggestions were made. Some were age-appropriate for my youngest, while I had a sneaky suspicion that others sounded a little more in line with my older daughter's taste and age. I valued big sister's ideas, so I obliged and did end up purchasing one of the recommended gifts. After all, the packaging did indicate that it could be age-appropriate for my youngest little lady.

Fast forward, I brought the gift home and my oldest helped me neatly wrap the cute peach haired doll that had matching peach glittery eyes. Birthday time arrived and so did opening presents. What started as a celebration of my youngest with playing games, eating her favorite food, and good ole fun turned into a pouting party by my oldest. Big sis wanted to play with the doll she chose for her sister and got upset when little sis did not want to share. She also began to express frustration that she was not playing with the toy properly. She went on to lament about the fact that her sister was getting so much attention. My husband and I gently reminded her that it was her sister's birthday, and we encouraged her to celebrate with her. We also shared that just because we were celebrating her sister, did not mean that we did not love her. She was even included in the party planning, game facilitation, and present selection. We went on to remind her that she gets celebrated on her birthday and other special occasions as well, but today was the day to commemorate her little sister's birthday.

Fast forward a little further, the night did not end well. Big sis ended up crying herself to sleep and sharing that her day had been horrible. I assured her that I loved her and that she was very important, and I even reminisced with her about the several parties she had for her very own birthday. My words did not seem to soothe her hurt, but I still attempted to help her understand the importance of celebrating with her sister. As I reflected on that precious time with both of my children, I was reminded of Romans 12:15 which states, "Rejoice with them that do rejoice, and weep with them that weep." Our Heavenly Father wants us to be able to celebrate and celebrate with one another in good times, and be able cry with our brothers and sisters when life gets challenging.

God, our Father does not want us envying or giving a side-eye when our brothers and sisters are blessed, because just as He has provided for them, He has done and will do the same for us. Sometimes the enemy tries to trick us into thinking that just because we see others receive a blessing, and by the way, it could be a blessing that you have been desiring that you have yet to receive, but your friend gets it first, that your new job, new home, new mate is not on the way. That could not be further from the truth! As a matter of fact, one reason to get excited is that if you see that Our Father is at your sister's house, that means He will be stopping at your door soon, so do not lose heart. He is God OUR Father! Just as I enjoy providing for both of my children, so does our Heavenly Father delight in showering blessings on all of His children at the appropriate time that He sees fit.

Can you think of a time where you found yourself feeling a little perturbed that one of your sisters, brothers, or friends got a gift that you wanted or had been praying for? Have there been moments when you have struggled to celebrate with others because you were looking to gain some attention in your own life? What are some of the lies that the enemy tried to tell you in those moments? Take some time to pray this prayer. Dear Heavenly Father, I would like to first say thank you for all that you have

already done for me. I give you praise and glory. Please forgive me for the times when I get discouraged and have struggled to rejoice with those who rejoice and mourn with those who mourn in the following situations: ____
_____ (fill in the blank). Please help me to remember that just as you have and can bless my sisters and brothers, you have and can bless me and take pleasure in doing so. Thank you for loving me unconditionally. In the name of Jesus, Amen.

REFLECT & RELATE NOTES

_____

_____

_____

_____

_____

_____

_____

_____

_____

_____

_____

_____

_____

_____

Lesson 27

"TIME TO SING OUR PRAISE AND WORSHIP SONGS."

After bath time, lotion, PJs, and prayer, aka "knees," my daughter and I sing several praise and worship songs that she requests, I select, or a combination of the two, prior to my exit for the evening. There are some nights when she does not feel like praying or singing depending on how her day went, but we still do it anyway. I am a firm believer in the scripture that says to "Train up a child in the way He should go: and when He is old, He will not depart from it" Proverbs 22:6. I recognize the power in our prayer and our praise! Similarly, I know there are times when I don't feel like singing, just like my child depending on how the events of the day played out for me. Nevertheless, we pray, and we sing.

While I undoubtedly enjoy our time of song and prayer together, do you know what makes my heart smile? I am humbly delighted and truly blessed when out of nowhere, in the middle of the day, or times outside of the allotted time for our praise and worship time, my little one begins to sing those very praise and worship songs unto our Heavenly Father on her own. The words she sings uplift me! Whether it is "Every Praise" (Hezekiah Walker), "Say Yes" (Michelle Williams), "Wide as the Sky" (Isabelle Davis), "You Know My Name" (Tasha Cobbs Leonard), "Make Room" (Jonathan McReynolds), or any other one of the plethora of songs that we sing every night, her songs of worship bring joy to my very soul. The atmosphere seems to shift when I hear her little innocent voice lift up the name of the Lord! This reminds me of how our very own Father, God must feel when we sing praises unto His name and belt out songs of worship. All throughout scripture, our Heavenly Father admonishes us to sing praises.

Psalms 100:1-2 says, "Make a joyful noise unto the Lord, all ye lands. Serve the Lord with gladness: come before His presence with singing." Psalm 135: 3 states, "Praise the Lord; for the Lord is good: sing praises unto His name; for it is pleasant." Psalm 147:1 states, "Praise ye the Lord: for it is good to sing praises unto our God; for it is pleasant; and praise is comely." Additionally,

Psalm 149:5 states, "Let the saints be joyful in glory: let them sing aloud upon their beds." The common theme in all of these passages is to SING PRAISES! There is abundant power in our praise and worship. Not only do our praise and songs please our Father but our worship has healing benefits for our very souls.

What songs of praise and worship can you sing unto the Lord? If you find that you have had a rough day, sing anyway. If anxiety and stress are weighing you down and keeping you up at night, sing. If you are happy, sing. If you are burdened, sing. If you are winning, sing! Take some time to pray this prayer. My God, my Father, thank you for my life and every opportunity that I have to sing songs of praise and worship to you. You deserve all of my praise and worship. You have been so good to me. Please forgive me for the times when I struggle to sing, and please help me through those times. I pray that my songs are sweet fragrances to your nostrils and pleasant music to your ears. I adore you. In the name of Jesus, Amen.

REFLECT & RELATE ACTIVITY: MY TOP 10 PRAISE AND WORSHIP PLAYLIST

Take a moment to list your top songs of praise and worship. You can even use this space to write down some of your lyrics of praise and worship as well.

1._____

2._____

3._____

4._____

5._____

6._____

7._____

8._____

9._____

10._____

REFLECTIONS

My brothers and sisters, were you able to see that God IS your Father? Did you hear Our Father speaking through each phrase? Did the words spoken to my child resonate with your heart and connect with your spirit so that you could catch a glimpse of what He is speaking directly to you? My prayer is that through Part II you were reminded that you are who God says that you are. I hope that you were reminded that God works on His time, and that means that He is always on time even when life feels like He is not moving fast enough. I hope that you are able to see that God is your protector, your help, your disciplinarian, and your guide. God is your teacher. God loves you unconditionally. God is patient with you and nothing can separate you from His love. God is your biggest cheerleader and you can do all things through Him. He delights in your praise, worship, thanksgiving, and attitude of gratitude. Despite your flaws and sins, He never gives up on you and is waiting with open arms to receive you when you come humbly before Him with a repentant heart.

Let us pray. Dear God, my Father, thank you for speaking to me through your Word. Thank you for reminding me that you are my Father. Thank you for never leaving me or ever giving up on me. Thank you for being my guide and my teacher. Thank you for your discipline even when it is uncomfortable, because I know that you chasten those who you love. Thank you for reminding me who I am in you. Please continue to reveal yourself to me as my Father and remind me that I am your child. Continue to let me remember that with you as my parent, I cannot fail. I am in the very best hands. Help me to make you proud with all that I say and all that I do because I want to please you. I do want to hear you say, "Well done!" Help others to see your reflection in me and catch a glimpse of you so that they can know that you are Our Father indeed. You are truly an awesome Father, I love you, and I give you all of my praise. In the name of Jesus, Amen.

CONCLUSION

As we reach the end of this journey together in this book, I hope something was written or revealed that gives you a glimpse of God Our Father and reminds you just how very much our Heavenly Parent, God, our Father loves you. He wants what is best for you, and He wants to be close to you. I also would be remiss to not offer Christ to anyone of you reading this book who does not already have a personal relationship. The Bible says in John 14:6 "Jesus saith unto Him, I am the way, the truth, and the life: no man cometh unto the Father, but by me."

In order to have free access to your Heavenly Father, God, I extend an invitation to accept Jesus Christ as your Lord. John 3:16 states, "For God so loved the world, that He gave His only begotten Son, that whosoever believeth in Him should not perish, but have everlasting life." Your Heavenly Father gave His only Son so that you might be saved. He loves YOU just that much. So, I hear you asking, "Well what do I need to do to be saved?" That is a phenomenal question! Romans 10:9 states, "If you declare with your mouth, "Jesus is Lord," and believe in your heart that God raised Him from the dead, you will be saved." Let me walk you through even further: 1) State out of your mouth that Jesus is Lord; 2) Believe in your heart that He died on the cross for your sins and God raised Him from the dead; 3) You are now saved! And yes, it is that simple. I am so proud, and so is God Our Father, that you are taking such an awesome and important step in your life!

Let us pray. Dear Father God. You are such a loving and good Father. Thank you for sending Jesus to die on the cross for me. Thank you that He rose from the dead for me. I confess my sins, I turn from my sins and turn to you and ask that you please forgive me. I am committing my life to you right now. Thank you for saving me. I am grateful for free access to you through prayer and the Holy Bible. Thank you for all that you have done, are doing, and will do as I give my life to you right now. In the name of Jesus, Amen!

If you just prayed this prayer, I encourage you to connect with one of your local churches where you can continue to learn more about God, our Father, more about God the Son, who is Jesus, and God, the Holy Spirit who dwells within us. I am so excited and count it a privilege to have shared this journey with you. I pray that after having read this book you were able to catch a glimpse of God, Our Father through each reflection, note, and activity, and experience feelings of hope, joy, and peace as a result of each gentle reminder. Thank you for taking this journey with me! I will close with one of my favorite scriptures that is found in Numbers 6:24-26 which states, "The Lord bless you and keep you; the Lord make His face shine on you and be gracious to you; the Lord turn His face toward you and give you peace."

Please visit the appendix where I have also included some other traits of a parent, but most importantly our Heavenly parent, God, Our Father with scriptures that highlight the characteristics.

For those who have been blessed to have positive interactions with fathers, some of the characteristics listed will sound very familiar. As with our earthly fathers (and mothers), many of the following qualities and traits have been showered upon us. Please note that this list is not exhaustive, but rather includes many of the qualities of our earthly parents and more importantly provides a glimpse of Our Father, God.

Fatherly/Parental Characteristics

Caring - 1 Peter 5:7 states, "Casting all of your care upon him; for he careth for you."

Compassionate/Comforter - 2 Corinthians 1:3 states, "Blessed be the God and Father of our Lord Jesus Christ, the Father of mercies and God of all comfort."

Disciplinarian - Hebrews 12:5-6 states, "My son, do not make light of the Lord's discipline, and do not lose heart when He rebukes you, because the Lord disciplines the one He loves, and He chastens everyone He accepts as His son."

Encourager - 2 Thessalonians 2:16-17 states, "May our Lord Jesus Christ himself and God our Father, who loved us and by His grace gave us eternal encouragement and good hope, encourage your hearts and strengthen you in every good deed and word."

Forgiving - 1 John 1:9 states, "If we confess our sins, He is faithful and just to forgive us *our* sins, and to cleanse us from all unrighteousness."

Guide/Teacher - Psalm 23:3 states, "He restoreth my soul: He leadeth me in the paths of righteousness for His name's sake." Psalm 32:8 states, "I will instruct thee and teach thee in the way which thou shalt go: I will guide thee with mine eye." Psalm 48:14 states, "For this God is our God for ever and ever: He will be our guide even unto death." 2 Timothy 3:16-17 states, "All scripture is given by inspiration of God, and is profitable for doctrine, for reproof, for correction, for instruction in righteousness: That the man of God may be perfect, thoroughly furnished unto all good works."

Helper - Isaiah 41:13 states "For I am the Lord your God who takes hold of your right hand and says to you, Do not fear; I will help you."

Love - 1 John 4:8 states, "He that loveth not knoweth not God; for God is love." 1 Corinthians 13:4-8 states, "Love is patient, love is kind. It does not envy, it does not boast, it is not proud. It does not dishonor others, it is not self-seeking, it is not easily angered, it keeps no record of wrongs. Love does not delight in evil but rejoices with the truth. It always protects, always trusts, always hopes, always perseveres. Love never fails."

Loving - John 3:16 states, "For God so loved the world, that He gave His only begotten Son, that whosoever believeth in Him should not perish, but have everlasting life." Romans 5:8 states, "But God commendeth His love toward us, in that, while we were yet sinners, Christ died for us." Romans 8:38-39 states, "For I am persuaded, that neither death, nor life, nor angels, nor principalities, nor powers, nor things present, nor things to come, Nor height, nor depth, nor any other creature, shall be able to separate us from the love of God, which is in Christ Jesus our Lord."

Merciful and Faithful - Lamentations 3:22-23 states, "It is of the LORD's mercies that we are not consumed, because His compassions fail not. They are new every morning: great is thy faithfulness."

Parent - Galatians 3:26 states, "For ye are all the children of God by faith in Christ Jesus." Psalm 24:1 states, "The earth is the LORD's, and the fullness thereof; the world, and they that dwell therein." 2 Corinthians 6: 17-18 states, "Wherefore come out from among them, and be ye separate, saith the Lord, and touch not the unclean thing; and I will receive you. And will be a Father unto you, and ye shall be my sons and daughters, saith the Lord Almighty." Genesis 1:27 states, "So God created man in His own image, in the image of God created He Him; male and female created He them."

Powerful - Ephesians 3:20 states, "Now unto Him that is able to do exceeding abundantly above all that we ask or think, according to the power that worketh in us."

Present - Psalm 139:7-12 states, "Where can I go from your Spirit? Where can I flee from your presence? If I go up to the heavens, you are there; if I make my bed in the depths, you are there. If I rise on the wings of the dawn, if I settle on the far side of the sea, even there your hand will guide me, your right hand will hold me fast. If I say, 'Surely the darkness will hide me and the light become night around me,' even the darkness will not be dark to you; the night will shine like the day, for darkness is as light to you."

Protector - Psalm 91:14-15 states, "'Because He loves me,' says the Lord, 'I will rescue Him; I will protect Him, for He acknowledges my name. He will call on me, and I will answer Him; I will be with Him in trouble, I will deliver Him and honor Him.'"

Provider - Philippians 4:19 states, "But my God shall supply all your need according to His riches in glory by Christ Jesus."

Sacrificial - John 3:16 states, "For God so loved the world, that He gave His only begotten Son, that whosoever believeth in Him should not perish, but have everlasting life."

Strong - Psalm 24:8 states, "Who is this King of glory? The LORD strong and mighty, the LORD mighty in battle."

Trustworthy - Proverbs 3:5-6 states, "Trust I the LORD with all thine heart: and lean not unto thine own understanding. In all thy way acknowledge him, and he shall direct thy paths."

Wise - Jude 1:25 states, "To the only wise God our Saviour, be glory and majesty, dominion and power, both now and ever." Isaiah 55:8-9 states, "For my thoughts are not your thoughts, neither are your ways my ways," declares the LORD. "As the heavens are higher than the earth, so are my ways higher than your ways and my thoughts than your thoughts."

Wealthy - Psalm 24:1 states, "The earth is the Lord's and the fullness thereof; the world, and they that dwell therein." Psalm 50:10 states, "For every beast of the forest is mine, and the cattle upon a thousand hills."

THE LORD'S PRAYER

After this manner therefore pray ye: Our Father which art in heaven, Hallowed be thy name. Thy kingdom come, Thy will be done in earth, as it is in heaven. Give us this day our daily bread. And forgive us our debts, as we forgive our debtors. And lead us not into temptation, but deliver us from evil: For thine is the kingdom, and the power, and the glory, for ever. Amen.

Matthew 6:9-13